THE GANGRENE
CONSTITUANCY

BY MICHAEL J GLEASON

THE
GANGRENE
CONSTITUANCY

MICHAEL J GLEASON

THE GANGRENE CONSTITUANCY
Authored By MICHAEL J GLEASON

ISBN-10 0615411576
EAN-13 9780615411576.

PREFACE

At the onset of this writing, I thought it would be enjoyable. As time passed it became apparent that my thoughts were rapidly changing from an optimistic outcome to one of gloom and doom. It soon becomes an undesirable endeavor. Nowhere does an attempt exist to convenience anyone to have a change of thought. Believe what you wish. I point this out because in conversations with people, statements were made for me to expand on my information base, so as to convince them of my position. I adamantly said that I did not care to convince them. Any attempts at selling an individual point of view, will not change anything.

There may be follow up of future developments which may prompt a second printing. This is not a current events endeavor; however it has to stand on its own merits as of November 2010.

Many inputs contained in this book have come from conversations with people around the world. This included a plethora of people in a variety of situations. The bibliography could have been much longer. Information was taken from many sources.

My background is varied. I do claim to have (non expert) knowledge in many areas. This does not make me an expert. Rather, just a person absorbing the many experiences of life. One of my work experiences was in many areas of the medical field, even in the area of Research and Development. This was over twenty years of experience. Not one year of experience twenty times. Thus, I believe that my inputs and ideas into the medical system would have a decent degree of credibility. The U.S. has the best medical system in the world. It has staffs, obviously including Doctors and Nurses, who work day and night with dedication. There is no doubt, that a system this large needs constant updating, and changes, which are designed to provide a broad spectrum of care to the population. The goal of reaching for optimal atainment is not achieveable by government bureaucracies. An optimal objective is not the goal of government.

Solely because of the Islamic terrorists, Muslims are derided in many facets of our civilzation. Methophorically speaking, if the shoe doesn't fit, don't wear it. It is apparent that more Muslims are killed by Islamic terrorists, than anyone else. This is not a double jeopardy type of thing. The vast majority of people recognizes this fact and is capable of separating out the terrorists and not stereotyping the Muslims.

I believe that if terrorists were removed from control of what is deemed to be Palistine, a separate Palistinian State could exist as a viable economic and sociological state, void of a violent conflict with Israel. Nowhere is there any indication of peace being a reality.

This book has a number of redundancies. Efforts to avoid repeating were not totally successful. Some sentences and phrases were used to reemphasize given situations. Also some information was scattered within different chapters. Each element was not screened and confined within specific chapters. It just would not work. In certain instances, parameters would be set restricting critical sentences. As such, the chapters may vary in length.

Certain people have sort of dominated specific situations.

1. Rush Limbough in citing the necessity of the Obama plans failing.
2. Michael Savage in reporting on the taking over of a port by Qtar.
3. Mark Levin by outling the vileness of the statists.
4. Neil Boortz in developing an awareness of the expansion of government, coupled with those dependent on government programs.
5. Glen Beck for his work in gathering a giant sized group into Washington D.C. and inculcating religious aspects.
6. Shawn Hannity for expressing a plethora of "conservative" views.

The preceeding is, obviously, not near an all inclusive list.

DEDICATION

I guess every book should have a dedication. For what it is worth, I wish to dedicate this book to:

The many Government employees, who despite the numerous obstacles placed in their path, somehow set out to work for us citizens

Along these lines is a special dedication to the military, many of whom continually risk their lives. In view of continuous deployment it is a wonder how they can ascribe to maintaining sanity.

CONTENTS

CHAPTER 1

THE GANGRENE CONSTITUENCY: VOTERS WITHOUT LOBBYISTS

The United States Is The strongest country in the existence of the earth. Our elected officials and their assistants have a predisposition toward sabotaging the citizenry. They portray other countries as giants being mistreated by the United States. There are constant unchanging factors like the United States making world wide mistakes, which for some strange reason have had negative effect on these societies. The energy crises is fostered by this group who envision us as not being able to drill for oil, construct nuclear plants or coal plants. Couple this with the environmentalists and the ever growing falsehoods of global warming that are paramount in handing over a plethora of dollars for imports of petroleum and other energy related products.

The United States cannot survive this government onslaught.

A people whose government is gyrating toward socialism and communism are, at least, at the moment unable to respond. A socialistic system will inevitably fail. It always has. An ever looming danger is the swinging of the pendulum beyond socialism to communism.

The decreasing of our freedom has been proceeding over a long period of time. It is now reaching a crescendo. Everything is coming together for the left wing radicals. With the alarms sounding, experts expound and threaten to pursue the same failed programs.

Many believe it is only government that can help the masses and solve the multitude of problems. An intricate look at this reality reveals that the government is unwilling and unable to accomplish much. In fact government is moving at an ever increasing pace in the opposite direction.

Greed and spite work are in abundance. The radical left (secular progressives) has a strong desire to totally destroy our system - politically, sociologically, economically, and militarily,

Quoting from Porter Stanberry, a stock market analyst, writing in his newsletter on October 29, 2009:

"One of the most important things to remember about socialism is it fails eventually because human beings have an innate desire for liberty and a strong need for personal rights. In fact, the origins of government lie in the need of agricultural communities to protect themselves from violence and theft. So it is particularly ironic that in more recent times, it is government itself that has more frequently played the role of bandit. When you start taxing people at extreme rates to pay for socialists benefits, when you start telling them which schools their children must attend, when you start giving jobs away to people base on race instead of ability...you quash human freedom, which bogs down productivity...and if continued leads to social collapse."

Take a look at the bankrupt State of California, where the productive people are leaving. The population increases are coming from illegal aliens and others who thrive on government assistance. New York is doing the same. Detroit could lend itself to a model of disaster. Pandering to the poor became an obsession. Government programs, demanding, among other things, what people should do, became a disaster. The incessant high taxes and loss of jobs caused a significant segment of the population to leave. Take a close look at Camden, New Jersey and other cities within the U.S. that have used the same liberal approaches toward problem solving. The tax base, coupled with a deteriorating economy, provided a picture of the results of government plundering. Under the stimulus plan, the State of California received five and one half billion dollars for education. Where did the money go? In early March of 2010, a multitude of "marches" took place in California dramatizing the plight of education.

- tuition was being raised by significant percentages
- class availability was decreased
- minorities were placing emphasis on how it negatively affects their educational motivations
- class sizes were increased as teaching staff was decreased

This is quite a display of incompetence.

Should one disagree with President George W. Bush, to the magnitude of undermining any of the programs or initiatives? This results in a major negative and as such is a disservice to the constituencies.

On the surface it can very well be eluded that the government is a wandering generality, without clearly defined objectives and initiatives. Inaccurate appearances are deceiving and treacherous. The citizens do not have a voice in the complexities of government. In fact it is the opposite. The current government operates against the interest of our people. Government perhaps even thrives over operating in the panic mode. It causes people to approach the public institutions for help.

A leader cannot absorb a single subject at the expense of other matters. The total systems concept and cause and effect relationships are not considered. Thus, crisis management is the call of the day. A particular example along this line is the concentration on the Iraq war in lieu of the emergencies in Afghanistan. It didn't happen. Concentrations have consistently been directed toward both wars. It is not ironic that when the total systems concept was in play, that the politicians contended that the Afghanistan problem was not a part of the war equation.

All the culprits are in lockstep. Each individual, for example, expresses the identical list of subjects, pro abortion, socialized health care, public health enhancements, jobs for illegal aliens, and health care for illegal aliens. Thus, for the most part, the government is continuing in its endeavors to control its citizens.

Consistent are attacks on the President Bush. Easily a conclusion can be reached that there exists a desire for the United States to lose the war on terrorism. Bill O'Reilly, as a guest on the Letterman show asked if he (Letterman) wanted the United States to win in Iraq. O'Reilly did not receive a response. This is not differentiated, in the reasonable mind, from treason. It is readily apparent that the personal attacks encompass much more than the war conflicts.

Education is sinking. There is a call for more funding. Student's academic achievements are falling below third world countries. These same failing programs are being repeated, while at the same time becoming more expensive. Something that works, like voucher programs, are scorned. The voucher programs give parents a choice as to which school to send their child. It invites competition. No wonder it is considered distasteful. To the liberals, it is a no brainer, merely stay on the same path. The benefactors are not the students, but the giant sized teachers union and those desiring to control the population. As of October 2010, approximately one quarter of the public school children were illegal or children of illegal aliens.

The Iraq war becomes immediately unpopular to the liberals. Senator Joe Lieberman, an ultra liberal, was ostracized from his party because he did not oppose the Iraq war. He won reelection in Connecticut by running as an independent. The liberals cannot hide from the obvious. Somehow there is an attempt to argue for defeat, only it is phrased as redeployment of military forces. A finger is pointed toward Afghanistan. This country as the propaganda is disseminated has been neglected. This is now the real source of our battle. Attention to a total systems concept voids the notion that one can wage war on the enemy in Iraq to the detriment of Afghanistan. Nowhere is it ascertainable, that the total systems concept is always operation. Indeed from mere observation, it is readily apparent that careful attention is not paid to the enemies in both countries.

Iraq is not a country to unite. Divisions, extending over hundreds of years, are not to be reconciled. Christianity is under constant attack. At the current rate of programmed deterioration, it will not take too many years before Christianity will no longer existent in Iraq. How then can a democracy exist? No doubt continuing efforts are being made in that direction. The broken promises in Iraq are many. For instance, the war was to be paid out of the sale of oil by Iraq and free elections were to provide for a stable government.

The success story is in the Kurds being able to progress enough to develop their own area. This includes profitable economic operations, coupled with and a large degree of stability. Meanwhile the Sunnis and the Shiites continue to wage war against each other. The government cannot even develop a viable working entity to include these opposing interests.

It wasn't that the U.S. went to war. It was that the U.S. placed impossible objectives in the path. The U.S. won the war, but did not develop a realistic plan to build a democratic government - even if it wasn't achievable. The let up or restrictions on force, analogous to Afghanistan, resulted in a loss of control over objectives and left the U.S. extremely vulnerable.

Individuals not have the influence they believe they have. The assumption that our representatives in Washington act in and for our public interests in any fashion is fallacious. Politicians do not act in the interest of the public. This is one reason why many legislators' have has a less than a 20% approval rating. They are for their own self aggrandizement. They also work feverously to establish and extend their power. In rare instances, these elements coincide with the public interests. Mendacious statements are a primary trait for the current crop of representatives.

Increasing taxes on productive individuals, inhibiting trade, controlling activities, enhancing the non competitors as in unions, protecting jobs while penalizing job expansion (not a paradox), crush optimism, etc… serve to create a sizable drag on the economy. The list is not all inclusive. However, it serves to create a basis for analysis in government actions. The crushing of optimism is less apparent.

Indeed the government is always talking in optimistic terms. It is the resulting realities that create conditions close to despair. Then it is government to the rescue. Only government lacks the ability to succeed. Regardless of their desires, the government's plans and programs find a way to fail.

One may seek solace and reinforcement from religion. Thus government is working feverously to undermine religion. Many of its formats are directed toward the youth, by way of disassociating the youth from the family unit. Public education is, like the economy, on a downward spiral. Government promotes and funds abortion.

There is the dissemination of false information and the recruitment (volunteering) of individuals to become politically involved. This is an insidious form of brainwashing. A cult like environment is perpetrated upon the unsuspecting. Volunteerism can become and end within itself. The volunteer strives toward an objective, enjoying a unique feeling of accomplishment. It takes away from a plethora of activities necessary for a citizen subscribing to positive economic contribution. Some primary examples are religious involvement, athletic endeavors, educational endeavors, employment, and family involvement. These must compete with the "other" culture that deprives the cult member of individualism and leadership. Characters are purposely developed to be subservient to the desires of the cult leader or state. Often we hear of community service-ditto for the convicted, which have their sentences ameliorated to perform in this atmosphere. There is a good side to volunteerism and community service. The upshot is its use by government to direct individuals toward its own programs and objectives. Also, when does volunteerism become mandatory? For example a child is not moved forward in the educational system because of his or her failure to garner enough volunteer credits.

The United States is fast becoming a Socialist nation. Socialists are diametrically opposed to Capitalism. Government is the answer to our being able to exist. A thin line, (more often than not, it is indiscernible), exists between Communism and Socialism. Marx in his philosophy set fourth dialectical materialism. Time and again we have heard such phrases as each according to his needs. An elitist group, with the power to grab all of the riches within their realm, and enslave the population is the determinant. It is paramount within such a vile system and must be stopped. A simply definition of Communism is an atheistic dictatorship form of government. Regimes, throughout history, have recognized the need for them to subvert religion. The masses cannot have reliance on anything but the State for their existence. Destruction of the free economy is planned in respect to gaining control of the population. Again there is a reliance on the government to provide. The constant message is that government holds the only possibility to proper existence. Historical evidence clearly shows free people healthily compete. Such persons are motivated to such a magnitude that they easily outperform other less fortunate, unmotivated, individuals.

Absurdity of government statements and actions extend to deleterious human results by curtailing motivation. The people in charge promote a state of fear via economic chaos. Any means to foster a welfare state, wherein people demand a multitude of entitlements without having to work for them. Among other elements, taxes are increased to further the desires of these freeloaders. The economy is further weakened.

Tax dollars and confiscation are used to promote socialism and, communism. Without being too much aghast, take a look at the individuals who surround Obama.

The year of 2008 depicts many critical incidents of the decrepit economical, social and political elements. The gains by the socialists in 2008 are staggering. The outlook manifests itself as gloom and doom.

The year of 2009 shows us on a speedy road to socialism. It is more staggering than 2008. Extinguishment of freedoms is rapidly approaching. The growth of government and its expenditures serve to dissipate any hope of capitalism having a paramount effect on the economy. Many of these taxpayer dollars will be used against the citizens of the United States. Just around the corner is government control over the work force, and owner-ship of many industries. This includes banking system.

The state governments are drowning with deficits. The higher tax states are in worse shape. Not ironically they are the entities providing the most dollars to the non working, structurally unemployed, and the work leeches that refuse to labor.

There is an income and capital crisis, not a credit crisis. Whatever, the results can be the same. As of December 2008, there is no place to hide. The downward movement is prolific, in this world wide situation. The government's actions to offset extremely negative dilemmas are creating more downward momentum and thus economic fear. Propping up the banks and brokerages houses that failed the system in the first place can only increase the problem. If nothing was done by the governments, we would stand a chance of survival.

The gang of operatives does not have any idea of what they are doing, except for those who are out to break the country and pave the way toward bankruptcy. Never in the history of the United States, has such outrageous actions prevailed. The outlandish spending of $ 700 billion dollars is not only doomed to failure, but could bring the entire economy tumbling down and send a gigantically strong country into oblivion. Add another $ 900. billion of borrowing, under the myth of being a recovery program, and the catastrophe comes into clearer focus. The same group that got us into this mess is being paid extremely high monetary compensation to get us out of the enigma by using the same methodologies.

Every day that government grows, it will cost the taxpayer more money and freedom. These government people are country wreckers. The objective is to grasp more power and undermine the population... They believe only government can solve the big problems. Carefully note that it is they, in practically all of the instances, created the problems. So the crises creators who make life difficult for the constituency hold themselves out as the hope. One has to conclude that these government people are purposely incompetent.

The mode of recent operations promotes the law of unattended consequences, which ends in disaster. Suppose it is intended? The policies are just carried out with reckless abandon. The past administrations are to be held responsible for the failures. Accomplishments are applauded and credited to President Obama. Since accomplishments of substance are not existent, the Obama Administration distorts the deleterious programs by promoting them as future successes - a reach for elusive hope.

Brain washing techniques extend too many areas of the system. With the economy progressing into depression, there are broad orchestrated positive predictions providing hope for the future. However, as time passes and the predictions fall far short of expectations, hope rapidly dissipates, along with the disintegration of motivation. The future determinants of hope turn to despair. Inevitably only those who envisioned the reality are spared from deep depression. The government continually paints an optimistic outcome. It is an unachievable goal.

Homeland Security was constructed as a gigantic government coordinated effort to thwart our enemies and provide added security. Why it was even suggested that a nation like the United States needs such control at the top? Along comes another generated organization that is void of any necessary function. All of these tasks are addressed and performed by the various agencies. The suggestions came out of a government committee to practically assure us in the aversion of another 9/11 incident. Homeland Security's actions after its formulation are deplorable.

1. No stereotyping of individuals - not political correct.
2. Open borders. Terrorists can enter the United States with impunity.
3. Apologize to the Arab Nations for any actions which may be deemed inappropriate - void of any thing that may protect our borders.
4. Place restrictions on the citizens of the United States.

As if this is not sufficient within itself, along come those who would like to create another bureaucratic entity and simultaneously make it a cabinet post. This has to shape up as another element in the lock step approach promulgated by the government radicals. Lewis Diuguid in a commentary published in the Kansas City Star on November 30, 2009, stated that a peace department is long overdue. He portrayed it as strength, and not a weakness. Not withstanding that at each and every chance, the enemy dramatizes its hatred for the free Islamic world.

To quote Diuguid:

"A peace department would ensure that individuals who want to serve the nation as Hasan once did would find the appropriate, stable spot during their time in the service. If identified to be mentally unstable, those individuals would be removed immediately to receive treatment."

Hassan is the terrorist that killed 13 and wounded 30 people at Fort Hood, Texas. Was not this "spot" system already in existence and easily identifiable? Why would a peace department need to do this task? One has to be curious as to why this approach would be suggested.

To further quote Diuguid:

"For the military's purposes, peace standards for service personnel would mean that each person would put peace first for the safety of everyone. People in the service need to know they can trust and defend their fellow servicemen and women on and off bases and in combat".
"A peace department could defuse hatred that folks in the service might harbor just as it could have identified and addressed the boiling anger that Hassan had".

It is as though the peace department would face off against the military to obliterate internal hatred. It assumes hatred in the military exists and therefore is a hindrance to the mission. What about the enemy hating us?

Herein does the thought process of that desire to overload the government with useless agencies. This article is made a labor of contention because it sets forth a specific strategy within a plethora of non workable ideas that could culminate another sizeable expense for the tax payer, without any discernable positive return. Another criteria, is that its negative effects are probably far in excess of any (if any) positive effect. This is not redundant to the prior sentence. We are in a constant barrage of misinformation. The peace thesis obviates the fact that there are whose who hate the life style of Americans to such a degree that they are out to destroy not only the United States, but the entire Western Civilization. Constantly under attack are our religious practices, political institutions, et al. Hate is the key word. Seeking of peace is viewed as an innate weakness. Peace seeking attempts to absolve those who are actively employing methods to destroy us. These same lock steppers project us as the ones at fault and we should apologize for our actions. Appeasement is a prescription for disaster. Note, Neville Chamberlain's, " Peace In Our Time", which was most likely a direct message to the people of the Commonwealth as being able to achieve peace by appeasing Hitler.

In a later article, Duiguid mentions Ghandi as a man of peace. It was like he achieved his goal of peace in India. The divisions are catastrophic. Pakistan and India are bitterly divided and ready to launch an all out war over an innumerable number of disagreements, like disputed territories. There is no margin for error. Note that both India and Pakistan are capable of nuclear confrontations. Since the time of Ghandi, Bangladesh, attesting to the inability of people to "get along", has become a state separated from Pakistan.

The military has to get back to being the military and not be undermined by obstructions that thwart the mission. Specifically, the rules of engagement place combatants in added dangers. Politicians directing the wars (and controlling the generals), are incapable and do not have the ultimate goals in mind. The current military operations are absolutely essential. Winning the peace is not a military objective. Winning the war is. Any changes in the strategic objectives result in loss of U.S. military lives. Believing otherwise and setting up incompetent and corrupt governments, and expecting the military to fill in the blanks, are an enigma, which can only have catastrophic results. Now, if we had the proper peace people, they could solve these problems and the military could go home.

It is not that the American public is against the war. Americans want a victory. This is in contrast with foot dragging, horrific decision making, and formulating military operations within a restrictive structure of a non responsive, incompetent, and corrupt indigenous government.

President Obama is on board here. In the Hassan case, Obama warned the American public not to jump to conclusions. What conclusions? That Hassan is a terrorist who successfully targeted the military. With an innumerable number of missed warning signs, we are to proceed as though the Government will properly take care of things. Here we have a terrorist being provided with a lawyer, complete with Miranda rights. He is not considered a combatant. The actions and thoughts contained herein provide more that ample dangers to us. Again, don't jump to conclusions.

Diuguid, in a later article printed in the Kansas City Star lectured us on our in attentiveness to global warming. Part of the lock step approach. Now, "diversity" is added to the approach... It's like the population is neglecting a plethora of cultures, including homosexuals. The most likely agenda is to promote the idea that the main stream should feel guilty.

STATE OF THE UNION ADDRESS

Obama's State of the Union speech in January 2010, was an insult to our intelligence and mainly characterized by mendaciousness. To many it is a defining moment.

This umbrage, by Obama, with the Supreme Court's decision to permit freedom of speech in matters relating to corporations went over as a temper tantrum. In essence, as a result of the Supreme Court's decision, corporations would be able to make political contributions. Focusing on Obama's attempt to dramatize its displeasure toward any entity and not falling into lockstep with their objectives, is at best a portrayal of self interest objectives. At this juncture in our history, the Supreme Court is still within the realm of the separation of powers. A Supreme Court should not have an agenda. Its function is to determine constitutionality.

Cynthia Tucker in a January 31, 2010 editorialized in the Atlanta Journal and Constitution, concluding that Obama was not rude to the members of the Supreme Court, because he was right. So the attending members of the Supreme Court can be treated rudely in a State of the Union Address, providing the President is perceived as right. This is not withstanding that the contrived obsession is predicated upon an assumption that opening up the doors to enable corporations to contribute to political campaigns will solely benefit the Republicans. Thus, a conscience effort exists to restrict these types of political contributions. It should be noted that the Supreme Court decision permits Workers Unions to also contribute to political campaigns. Apparently in the past history of political contributions, Unions have not had any problem in this realm. This begs the question, how was Obama in his presidential campaign able to raise approximately one billion dollars? Herein is a bifurcation of the thought process.

In essence, the government cannot control contributions. The McCain-Feingold bill's efforts to thwart political contribution were, for the most part, unsuccessful. McCain in his efforts to offset any benefits to the Republican Party, although successful in the short run, was fruitless in the long run. Frankly, there is not a mechanism in the repertoire of government plans, laws and programs, to curtail the large amount of money spent on campaigns. Any attempts to do so have been circumvented. The magnitude of the circumvention was not demonstrated in the McCain campaign, where he stayed with federal funding in lieu of the private sector. This was one of the many self imposed obstacles McCain created for himself. Not too many years before, McCain conjured up with the Democratic Senator Feingold, to successfully formulate a bill to restrict campaign funding, which may have undermined the Republicans. Inadvertently, the Supreme Court decision, the instant case, somewhat repaired the negativism of the McCain - Feingold bill.

Cynthia Tucker made additional declarative statements to the effect that granting corporations the rights of humans opening the floodgates of influence, and foreign corporations being able to influence American electoral outcomes. This is simply not true. A foreign corporation, under law, cannot contribute to our political candidates. Actually, little is being changed by the Supreme Court ruling.

Additional, Cynthia Tucker alludes to a Republican takeover by extremists extended to being held hostage by the rapidly emerging tea party. How about the Democrat Party extremists, Nancy Pelosi and her quarantining the party members and holding secret meetings? This is the un-American way of conducting business by pursuing no compromising ideological objectives. Here is another example of the type of reporting that can be anticipated by a lock stepper.

Sarah Palin and the tea party people have apparently struck the Democratic Party fear nerve.

Nathan Deal, a possible candidate for the governorship of Georgia challenged the President to prove his citizenship. He was criticized by non other than Cynthia Tucker. Nathan Deal should have been called a Bertha.

Here is another antidote to closely inculcate into the message:

"Blame Republicans for using the filibuster to outflank simple democratic processes. That certainly is not what the Founding Fathers had in mind".

Of course it is exactly what the geniuses had in mind when they formulated rules to distribute power so as to protect the majority who at times are not property represented by the Senate? Here is a case where the Senatorial party in the majority decided not to vote the wishes of the majority. Thus the filibuster rule of the Senate worked for the majority of Americans. However, it was short lived, as the Senate procedures, inculcated into the system at the start of the Republic, were circumvented. A prime example was the passage on the dreaded health care bill.

The Democratic extremists are unable to find a common ground for working together with the Republicans. In analysis of the polls, they are committing political suicide. This is in addition to promoting a multitude of divisions within the system.

The Obama's speech included the punishment of banks by specialized taxation. These taxes would have to be passed on to consumers. Also, the government, in a punitive mode, would put in place a bureaucratic examining system to insure that the banks do not make risky loans. Another bureaucracy would be created. The financial institutions, in determining loan criteria, will be cautious. The legislation, true to form, will have enacted another detriment for the economy. Politically, it sounded really good. However, it was an admission that he was unable or unwilling to curb the incredible bonuses - in the billions. The bill later passed the House and Senate. If it were not for the government bailouts, the billions of dollars taken by certain executives, as bonuses, would not have been available. Thus, billions of dollars were provided to this segment of a corrupt system while exclaiming the absolute necessity of preventing a banking catastrophe.

How much of this is on purpose?

In the area of taxation alleviation, capital gains tax paid by small business is to be curtailed. Small businesses rarely pay a capital gains tax. They pay income taxes. Thus, we have another good sound bite for the "speech listeners".

Then it's the perennially tax the rich rhetoric. Increases in taxes do decrease economic activity and result in a decrease in revenues. There are reasons for this:

1. People find a way to pay fewer taxes.
2. Primarily because of uncertainty, the business community is void of motivation, and thus not inclined to create positive economic activity.
3. The money taken by government is used by government. It is taken form the private sector. The government created dilemma removes consumption expenditures and money for private business for equipment and payroll.

Judging from the State Of The Union speech, there will be an effort to create a jobs bill. The administration had over a year to create jobs. Obviously, it did not happen. The stimulus plan was not designed to create jobs. Somehow the name changed from a stimulus plan to a jobs bill. Sense the stimulus plan, obviously did not create jobs, it is alleged to have saved jobs.

Obama mentioned using nuclear power to solve a portion of the energy problems. Nuclear power is not a green energy. Therefore, we know that this is not a true statement. Permits for construction of nuclear plants are overly restricted. Again we have regulators marching to the tune of the administration - of which they are an inherent part. Some of the nuclear plants are up for renewal of continued operations. It will be interesting as to how this will play out. Nuclear energy is a powerful element in the efficient development and use of energy. Restrictions on their use are detrimental to the United States. Many countries are way ahead of us in the efficient use of nuclear energy.

The Copenhagen gathering was a typical program, wherein the organizers participated in a glaring failure. Many or our representatives attended the Denmark party, at a great expenses to the taxpayer. They did not accomplish anything. Not one of the attendees stood up for us Americans. Tyrants such as the like of Hugo Chavez demonized the United States of America.
The subject of global warming is presented as a proven hypothesis. Fraudulent experiments where scientists concurred with false findings are purposely overlooked. Many of the results were altered in an attempt to prove a false premise. The Anglican event in England left a team of these fraudulent scientists exposed. The altering of data depicts the length these people will extend efforts to promote civilization as the primary culprit of the environment. Here we have the prostitutes of the scientific community. They diminish the creditability of scientists, and as such should be identified as having questionable credentials. No doubt this will have a harmful effect as to the efficacy of science.

Appointment of a commission to examine the government deficit was turned down by the House and Senate. Obama, not withstanding the fact that a commission like this has never worked, signed an executive order creating such a commission. The commission will most likely be employed to provide cover for the generation of a national sales tax (VAT) or value added tax, and other devious methods of reaching into the pockets of the constituency.

The impetus in the realm of our tax dollars used against us is unparallel in our history. It is designed along the lines of the lock steppers agenda to:

- Wipe out savings
- Provides bailout loans to the elites or the favorites
- Obama removing the word terrorists from the vocabulary
- Change Islamic terrorists to insurgents
- Destroy the private sector - death of entrepreneurs
- Provide desirable data and information from fraudulent science
- Fund loss of liberty programs
- Bankrupting the medical system
- Promoting illegal immigration-remove border protections
- Provide funding for reeducation camps (training)
- Socialize the banks
- Socialize industry such as in auto production and oil
- Paralyze unwanted initiatives by citing political correctness
- Inhibit progress at NASA by canceling vital programs
- Stifle the military by curbing the defense budget.

The perceived eventuality is a drastic change to socialism, characterized by the governmental promotion of sociological reliance's. The momentum cannot be generated with such force that it will necessarily stop at socialism. The pendulum could easily swing all the way to Communism, that is, total enslavement. Could this be the immediate goal?

The Nashville Tennessean on June 9, 2010 published an article called, Obama Joins Jackals against Israel.

"President Barrack Obama, who got his start in politics, in the living room of domestic terrorist Bill Ayers and Bernadine Dorhn, has spent his first year in office apologizing for American history".

"The populists, Tea Party member if you will, have already determined the policies of the administration to be defeatist. This is domestic and global. Many of the inhabitants are clinging to the same lifeboat and believing the yes we can rhetoric. The pacifist solutions people, like the democratic Dennis Kucnich would like the citizens to believe we can love our way out of the many conflicts. This letting down of the guard, allows (among other things), Obama to undermine the military."

Government, regardless of its intentions, is incapable of managing big complex economies. The empirical evidence is overwhelming. Historically, a government controlled economy has never been successful.
Here are but a few of the reasons:

1. Government cannot efficiently allocate capitol.
2. The created bureaucracies to operate the economy lead to corruption.
3. The cost of regulatory compliance on business is devastating.

The communists stuck to a five year plan, which had no chance of success. One of the primary characteristics of the communist endeavors is that it did not create any significant innovations. Note that Cuba and the USSR were miserable failures.

Cicero- 55 BC, quoted:

"The budget should be balanced, the Treasury should be refilled, public debt should be reduced, that arrogance of officialdom should be tempered and controlled, and the assistance to foreign lands should be curtailed lest Rome become bankrupt. People must learn to work, instead of living on public assistance."

Cicero knew what he was stating. Taxes are not the answer. People have to be allowed to keep more of their money.
Washington is increasingly becoming a profit center for lawyers and lobbyists. This part of the private sector does not add desirable production to the economy. It is an example where government absorbs the private sector's energy. The efforts spent to influence legislation or protect their interests, could find better utilization, developing scientific or technological principles. Government is also taking over scientific experimental methodologies, such as stem cell research. Now pure research or research for the sake of research can lead to scientific achievement. It is not at issue that it

can provide paramount value. Cell research is or should be within the realm of private industry, not taken over by government. Here is where government invades yet another area. The scientists are somewhat controlled and no discernable results will probably be forthcoming. Private industry, unless it sees a potential profit or promise of scientific success, may not take the big leap into sizeable investments. However, private industry would not ordinarily overlook a viable investment situation.

A point of viability in the private sector is that a multiple number of decisions have to be thought out, if for only recognizing the requirement to compete and be efficient. Bureaucrats do not have to climb this "thinking obstacle".

FROM BUSH TO OBAMA TO MCCAIN

How did Obama get elected in the first place? Congressman Ryan was the heavy favorite to win the Senatorial race in Illinois. However, the fix may have been in place. Ryan was in the midst of a divorce. Allegedly he was involved in a sex scandal. As a result he removed himself from the race, paving the way for Obama to be elected into the U.S. Senate. The sex scandal never developed. It was later rumored that Ryan was absorbed into the Goldman Sachs organization.

A few years later Obama went to New York and met with George Soros. A couple of days later he announced himself as a Presidential candidate.

The selection of John McCain to run on the Republican ticket was a mitigated disaster. McCain is a genuine war hero. However, there isn't any transition of this into the political realm that extends to the constituents. Somewhere along the line, before the primaries in North Carolina, the press gathered behind McCain. Perhaps this was all of the impetus he needed to propel himself into the Republican nomination. Not withstanding the fact that McCain received fewer votes than in his previous primary contest against George W. Bush, eight years earlier. Yet, the press proclaimed him as being a big success in the Carolina primary. Every time during the presidential race that McCain showed signs of grasping the lead in the polls, he found a path to falter. The question arises as to how McCain could have established himself as a viable candidate.

McCain, to feed the coffers of his campaign, went for the federal funding. This was again another critical shortcoming. Without ample funds, it was all but impossible to compete. It appears that he shied away from the prospect of conducting a competitive campaign. Despite all of this cajolery, it must be noted that McCain has received over the years, a sizeable amount of money from George Soros. Thus, George Soros covered his interests on both sides of the fence.

In the end, the race was reasonably close.

CHAPTER 2

DIABOLICAL AGENDAS

Government In Its Quest To eliminate freedoms promotes a vast array of weapons. Here are a limited number of subjects.

FAMILY DESTRUCTION MARRIAGE AND DIVORCE

People are splitting up at a rapidly increasing rate. Thus, divorce is on a steep upswing. Government is involved in these failures - up to its neck. Once one of the spouses seeks out legal advice, the entire family is subject to hostile government interference.

Michelle Gauthier, founder Defending Holy Matrimony, recognized the government promoted devastation by verbalizing, "When that one spouse visits a lawyer, they place the entire family in the hands of a hostile court system. Children become wards of the state, and all marital assets are controlled by the courts. It is truly a tragedy." This was cited by David Kupelian in his book, The Marketing of Evil.

Studies show that the children have negative impact. The father is removed from the child's life. The psychological problems are severe - depression, poor academics, medications for mental problems undermining performance required for a normal existence. The child develops asocial behavior. The youth feels overwhelming pressure to conform. Limited in leadership, the youth becomes a follower where certain corporations, like Viacom, Disney and MTV, are able to sell billions of dollars of products. The marketing research is superb. It uncovered a distorted desire to conform, be ridiculed, and somehow cater to undeterminable values. It delves into the darkest part of the mind where sex, hated, and violence reign. Free from

God, they can make their own rules. In this subculture, all religions are equal including those that worship Satan.

This young culture, remote from the Judeo-Christian ethic, is caught up in the anything goes attitude. David Kupelian in The Marketing of Evil causes deep concern for our youth.

"Today's culture is so poisonous that your only hope is to literally create another culture entirely-a subculture. Just as today's homosexual culture, for example, used to be a miserable subculture lurking in public toilets and seedy clubs, but today has become the sophisticated culture of the 'beautiful people' and Hollywood, so must your true American culture-if it's ever to come back-begin again as a subculture." This brings us to home schooling, an actual belief in God, and family values and a subculture designed to retrieve the natural elements of a reasonable existence, and provide an on the front lines offensive against interventions by the moppets from Washington.

The frontal assault on marriage, by an out of control government, eliminates the father. The no fault divorce is a boon to the governments agenda. Look at this sociological dilemma as creating profitable centers for all of the involved professionals, e.g., lawyers, countless types of consolers, social workers, and other family support services activities designed to isolate the members of a once functioning family.

God is out of the picture. The husband, immobilized, is no longer the provider. Although he may pay alimony and child support, his role is relegated to a non entity as custody is assigned, by law, to the mother. The state is the perfect paternal substitute. However, children suffer the most in the dismantlement of the family unit. Without the father, crime and poverty become paramount features of the child's existence.

The deprivation of a father causes vast behavioral problems. Both health and grades suffer, causing asocial behavior. Many, even after extensive psychological treatment are unable to properly function.

The feminist movement characterizes marriage as slavery - a legalized rape. How could a self respecting person become so dependent on a "husband"? It subverts self actualization, and ruins self esteem. A wife is unable to pursue her career ambitions. In essence marriage should be abolished. The ambiguities and inequities between men and women dictate that marriage is oppressive and therefore must be destroyed.

Women also suffer from the devastating problems of divorce.

CHRISTIANITY: JUDAISM

There is a spiritual void in this country. The loss of moral strength is a victory by those hell bent on the United States being overtaken by radicalism. The failure rate of marriages for "believers" is the same as the general population. Many church goers believe in abortion, gay rights, and other varieties liberal multi culture aspects. There is a concerted search for "something" outside the church. For example, too many Christians believe they are "saved" and are guaranteed automatic passage into heaven. Therefore they can enjoy the decadent secular elements of the world and away from family and its values. The youth are remote from the guidance and supervision by their parents.

Contradictions in the world view of Christianity prevail throughout the world. A plethora of new churches has emerged in our modern age to lend itself to these individual temperaments, e.g., special church for homosexuals. The Lutheran churches even promoted a homosexual priest to Bishop. The National Council of Churches had adopted radically leftist ideologies extending to terrorists in Africa. (Ref. Marketing of Evil, page 219). Conservatives have somewhat impaired the funding of the National Council of Churches. Eventually, they found funding from other sources to continue their devious work.

These same groups side with the Palestinians terrorists against Israel. Some of the Muslims are indoctrinated at an early age to die killing the Christian and Jewish infidels. The reward of experiencing Paradise will be instantaneous.

No respect for God equates with no respect for self or other people. It leads to the evils of self destruction, persuaded by emotions, in lieu of reason. Christians, lacking knowledge and understanding, are not able to defend their faith. In their, book, "The Faith Given Once, For All", Charles Colson and Harold Ficket stated:

"Christians must see that their faith is more than a religion or even a relationship with Jesus; the faith is a complete view of the world and humankind's place in it. Christianity is a world view that speaks to every area of life, and the functional doctrines define its content. If we don't know what we believe - even what Christianity is - how can we live it and defend it? Our ignorance is crippling us."

Christianity and Judaism are under attack. Separation of Church and State is one of these constantly alluded to concepts that is cited to exist in the Constitution. It does not exist in the Constitution. The First Amendment states that, "Congress shall make no law respecting an establishment of religion or to prevent the exercise thereof." This is purposely misinterpreted by the leftist extremists as a reason to remove reference to or reliance on God. It coincides with the goal of controlling the population by taking the place of God. Many businesses are cajoled into removing merry Christmas from their "greetings" and advertisements. Prayer in schools is quickly extinguished and the Ten Commandments are forbidden in public areas. In one case a cemetery was prohibited from having a planter shaped like a cross because it would cause emotional distress. Another judicial impingement on the rights of conscience raises its ugly head against the laws of nature and God.

In 1930, the Anglican Church broke with the tradition of the condemnation of contraception. Many religions predicted that acceptance of contraception societal chaos characterized by divorce. Throughout the remainder of the twentieth century, the Catholic Church did not waver in its stand on condemning contraception. Not so with many other churches, who abandoned this moral principal, and actually advocated contraception.

Mohandas Gandhi, the Indian Nationalist, a Hindu, was well aware of the catastrophic effects of this element of moral decay. He stated:

"If contraceptive methods become the order of the day, nothing but moral degradation can be the result."

One of the primary Humanae Vitae, released by Pope John Paul II's, alluded to the need for people to know the truth about the damage contraception and other lies have wrought to our understanding of marriage.

Over the last 35 years, the government has spent over four trillion dollars on a variety of social programs designed to remedy ills which can be attributed to the use of human sexuality.

Encouragement and taxpayer funding for abortions are a vital element of government programs. Since the Supreme Court Case of Roe B Wade, in 1973, fifty three million abortions have taken place.

HOMOSEXUALISM

Homosexual infiltration of the Churches is part and parcel of the expansion of their agenda. Criminal homosexuality stems from pedophilia. A paramount organization promoting such pedophilia behavior is Lambda. Thus, the spotlight can be changed to include pedophilia.

The homosexual community in promoting its self aggrandizement by looking as a victimized segment of society experienced a setback. This was the AIDS epidemic in the homosexual community. The society has to constantly be subject to desensitization. They must be perceived as victims deserving of special protection under the law, e.g., hate crimes. Parlaying the crimes legislation promotes the Federal Government's agenda in grasping further power from the States, particularly (as a start) in regards to murder cases.

In relation to the dilemma of the Catholic Church, the homosexuals went to extremes to depict the offending priests as pedophiles. Yet almost all those raped, and otherwise taken advantage of, were teenagers. Had the Catholic Church taken the appropriate corrective actions, and called law enforcement for investigations, a large segment of the dilemma would have been solved.

The problem is world wide. The United States receives the greater portion of the publicity.

The Christian reaction of offering to providing assistance to the homosexuals to change their behavior is met with distain. The message suggests that being gay is defective. Why not? How can one turn their back on the lowest of life's transgressions - sadomasochists, leather fetishists, cross dressers, transgender and child molesters? Of course, this is a relatively small minority of the homosexual community.

Aggressive promotion of homosexuality extends to our entire educational system - grammar schools, high schools, colleges, and seminaries. In furthering their goals, they discredit anyone disagreeing with them. Indeed they are bad characters. As with any self interest group, the gay community has many agendas. Among its many tools is propaganda. It is used to legitimatize such elements as same sex marriages, abandoning notions of right and wrong, prohibit criticism to such a magnitude that it becomes criminal as in hate crimes and demand silence of god worshippers.

Beware of being called a homophobe or a bigot. Here again is another of the homosexual weapons used to control the "straights". In one study, selected at random, noted that 43 percent of the surveyed had over 500 partners. (Imagine the exposure to an innumerable number of diseases.) This is juxtaposition with the homosexuals, within the realm of promoting specific of their lifestyles, making baseless claims and citing higher than actual numbers. Ridiculous statements are set forth, such as making acquisitions that famous deceased people were gay.

These people can be very militant. On December 10, 1989, during Sunday morning mass, pro choice and gay rights people literally raided St. Patrick's Cathedral in New York City causing havoc.

There are a number of arrant agendas. Many homosexuals favor same sex marriages, even if they may not participate. It is the same for adult- child (intergenerational) sex. The depiction is for this abhorrence to be sold as morally acceptable and deemed as consensual love. It is as a civil right extended to young children to engage with adults. This sets forth yet another element to demonize western culture. Knowing individuals and those able to exercise moral judgments and determine friend from foe, and good from evil. We are very well aware of the existence of evil in the world. For a viable philosophical thought, consider that without seeing evil, one cannot see well. Those able to exercise moral judgments are an enigma to those who pursue the agenda by promoting mind control and accuse the non conformist to their lifestyle as "hate" people. The out of control liberals have relished in the passage of a hate crimes law. What protection could the hate crime law provide to a victim of murder? More aptly, could this invite the federal government into the affairs of the state?

A demonstration of strength came federal court ruling in California, wherein Judge Vaughn Walker ruled in favor of same sex marriage, predicated upon a concocted constitutional matter referencing the 14th Amendment of the Constitution. The 14th Amendment has nothing to do with sexual preferences. The convoluted conclusion of the court came even though the California voters expressed views against same sex marriage.

This is another element extending diversification and dissipation of strength. In unity there is strength.

The AIDS epidemic, instead of depicting the homosexual community as promoting the disease, turned into an opportunity of presenting them as victims. Thus, there is an objective of developing a need for special privilege, which extends to entitlement to legal social rights above those in the normal population. Shaping the terms of the debate will culminate in advancing the gay agenda's, and provide the impetus of conjuring up tales of denied freedoms. Aids is a self perpetuating disease. Essentially, we know it can be limited. Apparently the homosexuals are motivated to remove this anathema from the human race. The funding is overwhelming, expanding to global proportions. The dictators have their hands in the till. In South Africa part of the drugs are seized for resale by the drug traffickers.

However, George W. Bush, in providing funds for the diagnosis and treatment of AIDS in Africa, created a positive, and charitable, outcome.

The United States military is undermined by legislative efforts to promote homosexuality in the armed forces. The don't ask, don't tell concept is not acceptable to the promoters of homosexuality. They desire to overturn the current program and make it imperative that the military accept the homosexuals. The result will be devastating to the military. Imagine, for example, a military attempting to function within the framework of a hate crimes law, or the Chaplains attempting to fend off immorality.

CHAPTER 3

MEDICAL

MALPRACTICE INSURANCE

Doctors are sued with impunity. Emphasis is on efficiency in the providing of medical care. Yet it serves the Trial Lawyers Association in their mythical attempt to control negligence. Juries award ungodly amounts of money. It's like free money coming down the pike. Do these jury people stop to think of whose pocket the money comes from and the effect it has on the medical system. It is a tragic situation. It is not in the actual damages that the subject becomes negatively prominent. Punitive damages are a primary culprit. These damages are considered by the judicial system to keep the perpetrator from compounding the problem. Punitive damages also add gigantic dollars to the settlement. Lawyers acquire a significant sum of the settlements. This is an obvious element to the transference of wealth to members of the legal system. Thus, doctors are sued with a vengeance. The work necessary to limit these exorbitant payouts is non existent.

Many elements of the medical system are taken over by special interest groups. Now government, having failed to correct the inequities in the system, is hell bent on taking over the entire medical care system.

Doctors are caught between the public, the hospitals, insurance companies and the patients who they must serve. Doctors are not properly represented, e.g., American Medical Association. In fact they are sold out to the power structures. Not only are the Trial Lawyers out of control, but also the insurance companies.

The medical crisis is multifaceted. Many segments must be analyzed with emphasis on efficiency in providing medical care. A good start would be to recognize the out of control organizations which are devastating the delivery of medical treatment. What type of people can be acquired to attempt to solve these obscurely determined criteria? A necessary part of the equation is technology. The Government cannot begin to undertake this giant sized task. The track record is deplorable.

The insurance companies do not have a vested interest in properly serving the policy holders. If the insurers pay out claims in excess of their expectations, they merely increase the premiums. Since premiums are paid in advance, they can invest the money and calculate gains on the time value of money. This unfortunately is not the only insurance problem facing the medical community. There are too many. One must consider state control of the insurance companies and its implications, such as diminishing competition. Among the leftist goals is to have the Government eliminate the private sector, thereby removing competition and selection processes available to the consuming public.

Where risk management fails, government can take over. Some of the malpractice and medical insurance providers are located in Bermuda and the Grand Cayman Islands. They are not subject to many state controls such as minimum capital requirements and can avoid U.S. taxes. Using the foreign laws of the corporation's domicile offset some of the common benefits of the U.S. health system, illuminating the deficits of competitiveness in the insurance industry.

The disarray in the system works for the benefit of the self interest groups. Drug companies and their hired lobbyists are amazingly successful in providing a plethora of drugs. Many of the medications are harmful and should have never been prescribed in the first place.

Doctors are not entering areas where they are vitally needed, such as family physicians and private service doctors in rural areas. The list is not are inclusive. Specialties have proliferated. There are many more dollars in the urban areas. Surgeons, for example, are in the more crowded areas of medicine. More dollars can be commanded. The higher remuneration may result in questionable, unnecessary, surgeries.

Patients will pay for certain treatments regardless of the cost. A patient having urgent need of an appendectomy, will not consider the costs. This is inelastic demand. The natural laws of supply and demand fail to operate. The occurrences of this are readily apparent in Medical Centers acquiring the latest in technology to facilitate tests and procedures. Patients, who exhibit complicated systems requiring intricate tests in order to formulate a diagnosis, have to be appreciative of the availability of these methodologies. However, to pay for these systems, too many patients are directed to the respective area of the hospital or clinic. Often the consult, test or procedures are not necessary. Another reflection for consideration is the patient's disassociation from the costs of the treatment. Many of the costs are paid for by the insurance companies or Medicare or Medicaid. The costs are perceived as the natural evolution of the medical system.

Determining end of life care is not an area for a bureaucrat. There are an innumerable number of factors, such as the quality of life, costs, technological applications, etc. Modifications of the current system need to be formulated. Nowhere, is it indicated that it should be scrapped and a government plan be instituted. Actually, this applies to the entire medical system.

Medical costs were not in a runaway mode until government interfered. The high cost of medical care has a multitude of causes.

The top three causes are:

1. Tort lawyers
2. Illegal aliens
3. Drugs

It no longer reflects the inflationary rate. The government inflation rate reflects a minimizing of pertinent data to undercut the real rate of inflation.

Tort lawyers are invited by the government to make further inroads into the messy system. Already, when the defensive medicine costs are tabulated, the legal system accounts for approximately 10 percent of the medical costs.

A system is in the works to centralize patient's medical information. If the information compilation comes to fruition, patients will be deprived of privacy and controlled by the government.

Juries award gigantic amounts of dollars. Juries obviously do not consider that the money does not grow on trees. These winners' proceeds are divided among lawyers, patients and their heirs. A division exists between doctors and their patients. The malpractice environment, which is a legal adversarial position, destroys rapport between physicians and patients. All this is justified in striving for prudent behavior. In actuality, it increases the cost of medical treatment by necessitating defensive medicine and of course malpractice insurance costs.

States do not have the power to prevent insurance companies from operating as oligopolies or monopolies. Thus physicians and hospitals are compelled, in many states, to pay huge rate increases. Insurance companies justify the increases, because funds have to be set aside for future claims. The providers can generate rate increases by merely threatening to withdraw from providing malpractice insurance. Somewhere systems have to be developed to place restrictions on patients to recover gigantic settlements.

The insurance companies, reluctant to actually insure risk or pick and choose, use lobbyists, at the state level, to promote their self interests.

Conversely, insurance companies are over controlled by the state, which for their (politicians) own self interest, have developed a myriad of rules and regulations. The administration costs defy imagination. Here we have an exception to the federalist ideal of maintaining control within the states. Both the coverage to patients and the provisions of malpractice need to be defined by the federal government with the emphasis on competition, i.e. the free market place.

Some insurance companies sought to compete by attempting to charge reasonable rates. This was not sustainable. Profit margins for the average successful insurance companies are barely over 3 percent. Not much margin for error. Government is increasing its control over the insurance companies by requiring them to cover, for example, pre existing conditions. Without a corresponding increase in rates, the industry will be placed in peril. It will assure a public option. Actually, the public option will be the only one that exists. Then government can indiscriminately increase rates which the citizen will be forced to pay.

The blood money industry was created in the 1970s. An embryonic system evolved into a catastrophe situation for medical care. Some hospitals went bankrupt. Others attempted to compensate by not paying malpractice insurance premiums. In many instances, physicians were left holding the bag.

The crisis is further explained by entities being taken over by entities that are able to bleed them into extinction. A major player, and prime example, in the game was Teledyne's acquisition of Argonaut, a provider of malpractice insurance. Teledyne cooked the books, never considered future claims, and paid large dividends to Teledyne shareholders. The emphasis on ethics was eliminated.

Over regulations are killing many aspects of competition. Conversely, without rules and regulations within the insurance industry, competition will not exist (reference the Sherman Antitrust Act). Monopolies and oligopolies coupled with legislatures and lobbyists will gyrate toward their greedy tendencies at the expense of the consuming public.

MEDICAL DRUGS GOVERNMENT HEALTH CARE

The government is developing a crash program to compile medical data on its citizens. This deviousness is involuntary. It torpedoes its citizen's right to privacy. Thus the medical system is a government tool to compile private medical information. It is rapidly evolving into a socialized system, where this information can be used against you.

A cost crisis in the medical area has existed for years. Little effort has been exerted to correct the excesses. Some of the costs may be reflective of actual inflation in lieu of the government controlled data.

It is an understatement that there is a scramble to convert the entire medical system from the private sector to the government. It is causing many on the left to display themselves as radicals.

Many members of the media are joining the radical bandwagon in writing paragraphs bolstering up the need for a Government takeover. As with global warming, the message is exaggerated and eventually culminates in outright untruths.

Barb Shelly, writing in the Kansas City Star on January 9th of 2010, exclaimed that Obama and the Democrats have shown flexibility.

"They abandoned the public option. They've done everything except sign on to the GOP plan, which apparently is six isolated measures that health care experts and economists say wouldn't significantly impact the number of uninsured or curb rising health care costs".

Barb Shelly is the same person who wishes for the future taxes and expenses, to be borne by public, to be moved up. This change of the effective date of this segment of the bill will have even more money paid in advance. What happens when all of this collected money is not available for its intended purpose of providing medical care? So many other government programs, like social security, have had their funds diverted by the politicians.

Nowhere has the level of flexibility come close to prompting a discussion of the medical care bill. The absurdity increases when Nancy Pelosi tells a group in California to pass the bill and then they will learn what is in it.

Obama repeated this when he exclaimed that if you want to know what is in the bill, vote for it.

If the current tax cuts expire, the tax increases will tabulate at 2.4 trillion dollars. The added taxes and other methods to collect monies under the guise of the socialized medical program make the projected damages to the economy unascertainable. All of this coincides with the aspirations of the anti capitalists.

The decision making process, required for the proper functioning of a system is absent. For example, Kathleen Sebelius, Secretary of Human Services, is supposedly required to make thousands of decisions to just implement the legislation. No person, when confronted by these decision making monumental tasks, can possible perform with any amount of efficiency. In the free marketing process, inputs are made by an innumerable number of people. The process involves the search for optimization relative to the profit motivations. Employment is provided to individuals most likely to succeed in this realm of achievement. The probabilities of success are largely predicated upon both competition and the desire to demonstrate initiatives in a free environment. It does not insinuate that the objectives be pursued outside of reasonable regulations. What Government employees work in this type of environment?

DRUGS

The professional people who we rely upon can cause us the most damage. Many of the prescriptions are poisonous.

Prozac and Zoloft are among the current common prescriptions, unwittingly provided to patients for anxiety and depression. The counter indications depict the symptoms of tic disorder, dyskinesia, non repairable brain damage, motor sensory problems, excessive fatigue, and suicidal tendencies. This is not an all inclusive list of the treacherousness of these drugs. Obviously, FDA approval of these medicines is a grave error. The monetary benefits accruing to the drug companies are enormous. Again, the citizen takes the proverbial back seat in the government scheme of things.

These specific drugs are designed to induce increases in the serotonin levels. Approximately 4% of the serotonin is in the brain. Serotonin is primarily found in the stomach and intestines. Increasing the serotonin levels even by an infinitesimal amount will decrease the brain's dopamine levels and cause detrimental chemical imbalances in the brain.

Patients on the mind altering medication, for even a short period of time, exhibit these horrible symptoms. These are only the short term results. Long term studies on the negative effect of these drugs are non existent.

With the inevitability on the detrimental effects of these methods of treatment, why are they not condemned?

For many, primary care physicians are the cornerstone of medical treatment. They have to not only be aware of the counter indications of the commonly prescribed medications, but must inform patients of the risks associated with taking these mind altering drugs. The dependence on primary care physicians to remedy the situation has severe limitations. One of which is that there are not enough of them. Also, they may perceive the matter differently and conclude that the patient, given the severity of his or her depression, is being provided the proper treatment.

So far we have been talking about adults. What about the children?

Pediatricians are being cajoled to prescribe the same mind altering medications. The FDA being cajoled by the drug companies to grant the appropriate approvals. Eventually millions of children under the age of 7 will have wandered into the expanded pediatric use of the mind altering drug.

Many of the public schools have demanded that parents place their children on Ritalin to subdue what is considered to be overactive classroom behavior.

Attention deficit disorder conjures up a prescription for Ritalin, a mind altering drug that increases dopamine levels in the brain. Eventually, the child, as a result of these addictive poisons that target the brain, becomes apathetic and excessively timid. The trend of drugging children is increasing.

Michael Savage in "The Enemy Within" specifically outlined the dangers of medicating our children.

The counter indications of the antidepressants are vast and varied, depending on the patient - suicide, projection (blaming others), distortion of reality, failure to take responsibility (apathetic), and deterioration of the mental illnesses. As the symptoms manifest themselves in a growing negativity, the medication, that does not "repair" is increased. Signs of creativeness or inventiveness will identify a child, particularly males, as a candidate for Ritalin. Ritalin is a forerunner for the more powerful mind altering drug called Prozac.

These drugs are also prescribed to the military. The suicide rate in the ranks is increasing. A hypothesis needs to be formulated and tested to attempt to determine if there is a positive correlation between the psychological drug prescriptions and suicides.

Whether intended or not, these medications can promote the controlling of the flow of ideas in the educational process.

Senator John McCain introduced a deleterious bill to place dietary supplements under the control of the Federal Drug Administration. If successful, the FDA will legally be able further serve the drug companies by harassing the nutritional supplement manufactures under the Dietary Supplement Safety Act.

The military is in the prescription dilemma. There is more than an equal chance that the rising suicide rate, in the military, is directly proportionate to tranquil prescriptions. Many service members also receive pain medication. The two together can magnify counter indications.

GOVERNMENT HEALTH CARE

This legislation points out the ability of the Democrats to circumvent the U.S. Constitution and prioritize a Senate vote for a health care bill that the majority of the citizens do not want. The bill was not even available for the Senators to read. Yet they felt that it was imperative for them to vote for it. This is quite a conglomeration of people demonstrating their lack of consideration of their constituency. The legislation is without doubt the most dictatorial bill ever passed. Placing health care under the domain of the federal government, removes many vestiges of freedom. The provisions of the bill are unimaginable to a free society. For example, a citizen could serve jail time for not purchasing medical insurance. Thus, the government usurps another power by creating a sub system, wherein it takes money from an individual, and gives it to itself or, in certain cases, for the time being, to an insurance company.

Because of outrageous legislation, many of the Congressman and Senators will not be reelected. In fact many will not seek to be reelected.

The legislative passing, of the medical care bill, happened to take place on Christmas Eve. The vast negative implications are not seen by the majority of the people. Yet the majority is against the medical care bill. For instance, they do not want to pay for other people's medical care. Why should we pay for people who do not want to purchase medical insurance, or are here illegally or are malingerers who refuse to work?

Interestingly enough, Daniel Shorr, the recently deceased news commentator from the Bronx, New York, mentioned that the majority rule should rule the day. That is the majority in the Senate. How could a system exist that one Senator's vote could be so important that he or she could subject the Senate to blackmail? Such is the incident of the 60th vote. What about the majority of the people (80 %/) who detest the bill? Maybe Daniel Shorr could have explained this dilemma. The eighty percent who came to the forefront too late have to sadly recognize that the system already countermanded any expression that they could exhibit to derail the legislation. Never has there been a piece of legislation that manifested itself by so many lies. At the time of the Senate vote, the bill had not been submitted to the Senate to read. Debate to read even an addendum to the bill on the Senate floor was stopped. A Senate parliamentary rule that existed since the inception of the Senate was cast aside. A Senate parliamentary rule is an inherent part of the Constitution and as such is considered sacred.

Illegal aliens are covered by the bill. Indeed, they are probably on their way across the United States border in droves in anticipation of an extended handout program. They will not proceed to Canada, which has one of the worst medical systems in existence. The Canadian system is replete with denial of medical care (even emergencies) or long waits for care that we presently consider routine. All this is about to change - for us, not Canada. Medical care had to be rationed. Simply there are not enough resources to accommodate the vast influx of people. Bureaucrats will be appointed to determine the recipients of medical care.

This is not speculation. President Obama has already informed the American public of his objective of having a government regulatory agency dole out the medical care via selectivity and determine who is eligible for which specific type of care.

The cost of medical care will skyrocket. It will be beyond the means of working class people. However, they will be forced to pay these excessively high premiums. So will small businesses have to contribute to this insatiable system? It is a gigantic tax on the working class of people. The Internal Revenue Service has been selected to collect the fees. Imagine the fate of anyone not paying into the medical care system. Already it has been stated that they will have a jail cell awaiting them. The severity of this measure is drastic. In fact, many citizens have stated that they will not pay medical insurance.

The indigent and illegal aliens, who are sure to receive care, will not have to pay. To the Obama Administration, it is a major part of a program designed to destroy the United States program.

The United States has in place the best medical system in the world Nothing else is close. Yet it needs major changes. For example the medical insurance system needs to be revamped. It is over controlled for the prospective of laws and regulations that simply do not work. It is non competitive. Being void of competition is always a bad sign. The insurance companies should be allowed to compete. Being bogged down on matters as essential as not covering pre-existing conditions, or not having to pay for certain procedures because they can be considered experimental, is not helpful. It sets up a screen and thereby excludes a search for a meaningful solution. The problem becomes inexorable. Eventually, a crisis is formed and the Government steps forward as the only entity that is able to provide any type of a solution. However, instead of formulating a solution, the Government advocates a takeover at a more that sizeable cost to both the taxpayer and the economy. Prescribing the everyday operations of a free marketplace business and instituting controls in profit margins and wages is fascism. It simply does not work. Historically it has been an economic and sociological disaster. A free enterprise system thrives on its ability to make decisions.

The new era of medical care will bring about, a multiplicity of unmanageable compliances, characterized by volumes of paper work. Here is another example of regulations run amok. Over one hundred more government agencies are being created to monitor the health care system. Who can pay for all these additional costs? No problem - the taxpayer can absorb the phenomenal costs. Here is another nail in the coffin of the consumer, which will obviously add to the economic woes.

The citizen must pay up front for his or her medical care. The benefits will not start for over three years.

Compulsory insurance will hand over millions of Americans to become medical policyholders. Small business will either provide coverage or be fined. As time progresses, the fines will be increased. Due to the expanded cost of doing business, entrepreneurs will be unable or unwilling to create jobs. Eventually, the insurance industry, unless it receives government aid (like General Motors), will perish. The demands placed upon the insurance companies, without being able to increase rates, will insure, without government subsidy, will have to refrain from writing medical policies. Thus, the government will acquire absolute power as a sole source of medical insurability.

The legislation was being rapidly passed. The objective was to race it through before the masses can be alerted of the actions of the miscreants. The legislatures are not only passing the bill without reading it, they are approaching unparalleled circumstances. The bills are coming out of committees, which met in secret. The bills of over two thousand pages are not even available for reading. Then attachments to the bills are written with the idea of passing the legislation in its entirety without being read. Add another dimension to this - even if it was available, how can one read and interpret or understand the bill and its addendums? Then there is the time slot relative to the immediacy of the vote.

Dr. Berwick has been selected to head up the new medical care bill. He is to head the Medicare and Medicaid sections. Dr. Berwick is another one of the Harvard radicals who will bypass the Senate hearings and receive a recess appointment. One of his many aspirations is to redistribute the wealth or more factually, steal from the rich (and middle class). He presupposes that the poor are more in medical distress than the rich, and therefore, logically to him, in more need of medical care. The medical system has limited resources. Placing the millions of illegal persons into the system will have incalculable negative effects on the delivery of health care. Many medical people will find better careers outside the government controlled system. Those remaining can count on being overworked and stressed out. At the onset of this socialized medicine, care will have to be rationed. Government employees will make these decisions. Already savings have been the order of the day in Medicare. Specifically, costs or payouts have been trimmed. Some of these savings have come as a result of decreasing payouts to doctors and having the states fund Medicaid. Billions of dollars are to be saved by the government curtaining Medicare payments.

As all of this is unwinding, the propagandists, and others who join the fray, go about their everyday procedures of lying to depict the legislation in a favorable light. The health care bill destroys the willing elements of a system that provides the most superior health care in the universe. Of course the destruction of the system was the primary goal of the administration. This is not theory. The observations coupled with what the constituency has learned about the legislation are unmistakable. Those who lack the capacity of formulating a willing system are destroying the one that is in existence. If the legislators operated in concert with past methodologies and took ample time to review the innumerable proposals, it would not pass. The majority of the voting public is already outspoken on the health bill. They perceive the matter as being lacking in substance as it relates to improving their medical care. As the facts leak out, more people are in opposition to the health care bill. It can be projected that many of those voting for passage will pay a heavy price at the upcoming November 2010 elections. That is why with every passing week certain legislators decide not to face the voters. But for us citizens, it will be too late. Reversals are difficult, even if sanctioned by the groups in power. Thus passing legislation as fast as possible to offset opposition can have, as in the instant case, vast consequences.

Obama is way in over his head. One must wonder who is controlling him. The reality is, even if he desired to do the right thing, he would not have the capacity to carry out a program.

The administration claims that its medical program will save dollars. Look at the programs that are already under government controls. The Veterans Administration and Medicare costs are out of control. The effectiveness of the VA is on a constant decline. Medicare can look forward to having restrictions on its providing of medical care. It will be the bureaucrats who make these life determining decisions.

The purpose of the program is not for government to concern itself with the well being of its citizens, but to generate a gigantic power grab. Somewhere along the line, medical care in the United States could comprise over 40% of the Gross National Product. The projection is probably accurate. An offsetting factor would be the restriction of access to medical care.

A partial list of the scary aspects of a socialized medicine in the United States:

1. Unintelligible laws, rules and regulations.
2. Trillions of dollars in taxes. For example, a so called Cadillac tax on what will be considered a luxury insurance policy and a large surtax on taxpayers in the higher tax brackets.
3. Vast increases in insurance premiums.
4. Cut Medicare by $ 465. billion.
5. Cost of 2.5 trillion over ten years.
6. Government bureaucratic to determine which health plans have to be purchased.
7. The citizens will have to pay for abortions.

8. Medicare and Medicaid, the Government's initiated programs will pay for illegal alien's medical care.

9. Will invite increased malpractice litigation. Ridiculous, frivolous, law suits will continue to support the Trial Lawyers.

10. Failure to purchase medical insurance will result in criminal prosecutions.

11. Insurance companies will be forced to assume larger liabilities. Attempts to pass the increased costs to the insured will be thwarted by the bureaucrats. The insurance companies will be forced to pay for experimental medicine and pre existing medical conditions. No doubt this is a problem area which needs to be brought to some sort of workable solution. However, this should be beyond the realm of the government. Placing insurance companies in mandatory (fascistic) situations will eventually lead to their demise. Government insurance will be the only alternative. People will be forced to pay whatever is bureaucratically determined. A growing portion of the populace is in poverty. It is readily apparent that a segment of the population will have to provide insurance for that the poor and indigent.

12. Mandates, such as Medicaid, directed by the federal government to the states, will further the unbearable burden placed upon the state and local governments. An already heavily taxed segment of the society will have a portion of the medical care bill placed up on them.

The reality is socialized medicine will spend an ungodly (incalculable) amount of money. The Investors Business Daily published figures on March 23, 2010 depicting a 3 trillion dollar cost estimate over a non specific period of time (perhaps ten years) with an immediate 569 billion dollar tax increase. The totality will further push the U.S. into bankruptcy. The sequel is to reform the system by recognizing the private sector as the most efficient in delivering proper medical care.

1. Lifting certain restrictions, permitting the insurance companies to compete and expand coverage.

2. Decrease, by a significant amount, the punitive payout in malpractice suits via legislation.

3. Restrict the medical care of illegal aliens to emergency care. Why should the American citizens pick up the tab for those who are here

illegally? Given the amount of unemployment and numerous financial responsibilities, how can the taxpayers afford to fund this segment of the medical system?

4. Open up competition in the drug industry. For example, permit citizens to purchase their medications on the open market. As a regulatory suggestion, stop the Federal Drug Administration, from approving dangerous and unproven drugs. Physicians have to take the initiative and make decisions to scrutinize prescriptions in relation to risk-benefit ratios.

5. Undertake the difficult task of sorting out the necessary medical procedures and treatments from those that can be considered unnecessary.

Both drugs and other medical treatment is a sensitive area for physicians. The responsibility should not be delegated or usurped by bureaucrats.

This is just a short list.

Instead of attempting to change the current medical system, the Obama administration is obdurate in its objective to take over the entire medical care in this country.

Congress and the Senate have each developed their own legislative proposals. And each have developed bills what are over 4000 pages plus addendums or attachments of hundreds of pages. Once again, the Senators and Congressmen who voted on this bill did not even read it. In fact it was not even available for review.

At one time lacking the votes to send their version of medical repair as a constitutionally formulated bill, the Democratic Party leaders have attempted to create a subterfuge by conjuring up the fiction of a bill having achieved the status of a vote. Here is where the legislature made a dangerous move, thus illuminating an obvious case for petitioning the Supreme Court. The Court could potentially rule in either direction or outright reject the review of the case. If viewed as a precedent, future proposed legislation could be passed by obviating the vote process.

Arm twisting, intimidation, and bribery became the tools to pass the legislation.

Now that the bill has passed, a number of States have moved to petition the Supreme Court to rule on the Constitutionality of forcing its citizens to purchase health insurance.

The efforts to take over our medical care system are without end. What happens or what is next after the destruction of our medical system?

There couldn't be too many people on the planet that believe the government medical reform legislation will lower costs. All types of lies and myths are promoted to offset the desires of the majority.

The medical care program is just a means to expand the infringements of government and collect a large segment of taxes, which will, among other things, inhibit economic expansion. The jobs market is in turmoil. The percentage of the American population that is unemployed is unfathomable. Indeed it would even be higher, if the federal government did not expand its hiring. These do not produce anything. Instead they are on the receiving end of tax money, which should remain on the private side of the economy to create jobs. The Obama administration had endlessly demonstrated its anti business bias and is obviously against any type of private investment. It is a prerequisite of an anti capitalist.

The elected Latinos, particularly in Congress, do not represent our interests, or the wellbeing of their constituents. During the course of events, the Latino members of Congress held out their approval vote until a guarantee was forthcoming from the White House to make insurance available to the Illegal Aliens. This insurance is all gratis. Thus, it is the persons with whom they identify, and not the constituency, that most approximates their loyalties. This is part of the 30 million expansion of medical care to people who refuse to purchase insurance, or are indigenous "poor" citizens or illegal aliens. Those who do not purchase will have been incarcerated, unless of course they are exempt by poverty or illegal.

The medical care bill will create over 100 more agencies. We already have too many agencies within agencies. Every day we learn of a new one. The expansion of costs can be allocated to two areas. The agencies create a plethora of paper work, and the medical care providers have to comply by completing the paper work and forwarding it to the agencies.

Why is there a hiring of 16200 more Internal Revenue Services employees? This is enforcement against the population. Why now, if the main elements of the bill are not to take place for four years? It is part of the wealth grab or redistribution of wealth. The objective of all this is to totally overtake the country. With decreases in employment and subsequent economical activity, the medical system will become approximately 30 % of the economy. This should happen in a short period of time.

The health care bill ramifications are exponential. It is a gigantic tool in the hands of the government to destroy our country. Never has the United

States Government had such power, and it will be used against the citizenry with impunity.

Backroom deals, vote brokering, outright corruption, arm twisting, obviating many of the senate rules, and assistance from numerous government agencies to promote the propaganda are symptomatic of the "tools" used to promote an agenda when the majority are steadfastly opposed to it. For example the Congressional Budget Office made the fallacious claim that adaptation of the medical reform bill will create a budget surplus. The Congressional Budget Office is charged with the responsibility of presenting congress with realistic data. Here is another example of us taxpayers supporting civil servants who are sabotaging the system.

The momentum of the force may be unstoppable.

CHAPTER 4

EDUCATION

Pravda, the leading Russian newspaper, had an article in June 2009 pertaining too many of the facets happening internally in our country. All of the mentionable are detrimental to our continuing to exist as a recognizable country of freedom. Some of the multiples examples are: giving up freedom without awareness, and developing less educated people.

Government advances the notion that college assistance for poor students will lower education costs. These convoluted notions serve the misinformed to accept the utterances as truth. Numerous times they are dragged out as part of the government misalignment of the truth programs, a planned methodology emanating in brain washing (control).

A large number of higher learning institutions have endowment funds, which generate income. All of this is, for some strange reason, exempt from taxes. A quantity of these funds was to be used to provide scholarships for low income students. What went wrong?

University costs are increasing at a rate which is far in excess of the given inflationary rate. Many are inclined to elaborates, (the fineries in life) - a part of the elite class. This element is above the sociological - economic contribution. These people are over remunerated. Within the parameters of Capitalism, they would have to forego these excesses. The tenure program provides job security. Indeed, there is a positive correlation between overextended benefits and high college costs. Government provides more incentive for these economic disparities by funding portions of the tuition expenses.

Overall, our educational system continues on a downward trend. Each and every year, graduates have less academic stature than their predecessors.

As usual, it's all in the statistics. The U.S. student is not holding up in comparison to its international peers. The acumen is plagued by a system determined to promote the National Education Association agenda. In the 1980s, Government was aware of this problem. President George Bush made the statement that he would be the educational President. Obviously, it did not happen.

The national teachers' unions are advancing radical agenda's. The students are lock stepped into reliance on government. It's actually a perversion. It's a major part of the destruction of America.

The author and talk show host, Michael Savage in his book The Enemy Within, cited numerous examples of depravity within the educational system. The Kansas City experiment started in 1985. Federal Judge Clark was the catalyst behind the expenditure of 2 billion Kansas City dollars to build new schools over a twelve year period. The Judge integrated the school system by bussing students all over the school district. The student test scores would elevate to the national norms.

A think tank, the Cato Institute pointed out what the Kansas City taxpayer acquired for its two billion dollars:

1. Fifteen new schools.
2. Olympic-sized swimming pools complete with an underwater viewing area.
3. Full television and animation studios.
4. A robotics laboratory.
5. A twenty-five wildlife sanctuary.
6. A zoo.
7. Higher teacher salaries.
8. Reduced class sizes with a twelve- to - one student - teacher ratio.
9. "Field trips" to such far away place as Mexico and Senegal.

The program was such as disaster that the Kansas City School District lost its accreditation. How hard it that to do?

The CATO Institute reported the obvious:

Test scores did not rise.

The black white gap did not diminish.

Once again the taxpayer was out the money with very little to show for it. In March 2010, apparently to dodge bankruptcy, the Kansas City school board voted to close approximately one third of its schools.

Mary Sanchez, a columnist writing in the Kansas City Star (March 16th 2010), expressed her desires for national standards for education. This approximates the Department of Education's Race To The Top Program. Here is another example of a waste of money. What bureaucrat will determine the curriculum? Already, there are changes (controls) in the text books. The top of the subject matter was indeed valid. It concerned the Texas Governor Rick Perry omitting from the education curriculum the assassination of Archbishop Oscar Romero in El Salvador, a number of years ago, by a right wing death squad. Of course all murders at that time in El Salvador's history were blamed on right wing misgivings. Then up comes the familiar lock step approach in citing that the teaching about the death of Archbishop Oscar Romero might raise questions (negative) about the United States abroad.

In a previous article, she alluded to minority students being stuck in a Kansas City school. Imaginably, the connotation is that there is a lack of funding.

El Salvador emerged from the cold war as a nation that has popularly elected representatives. You do not hear from the left wingers, who promote the Latino world about the intended plight of the Honduran people and the quest to maintain their freedom. Archbishop Oscar Romero is correctly recognized for his efforts on behalf of the El Salvadoran people.

Where are these people when it comes to Honduras? Either they are hiding from reality or they are against freedom and democracy. The freest country in Latin America was within close proximity of being taken over by a dictatorship. No one in the Democratic Party came to their assistance. In fact, it is the present administration that actually took bold steps, along with Hugo Chavez, to undermine the democratic process and cut vitally needed aid, particularly in the area of education and medical care to Honduras.

Mary Sanchez attacked a person in Nebraska who did not want to extend free education in the Colleges and Universities in Nebraska to illegal aliens. There is a no brainier. Nebraska is substantially increasing their tuition for all students. Many states are doing this in desperation. The residents of Nebraska are already stretched on their property taxes to maintain the current education system.

The situation stretches in the desperation and frustration of the passing of the Arizona law. Here we learn of the desires of those who demand illegal alien support for what is purported to be the Dream Act. It would have the taxpayers pay for the illegal persons' college. Those who oppose the bill are said by the lock steppers like Mary Sanchez to have no spine. One of the persons she named as having no spine and cowering is John McCain. This is difficult to imagine, but true. It depicts the extremes of language used in this secular progressive movement.

Principles on Immigration citing the Bible as saying foreigners must be treated as your native-born. So it was written by Lowell Grisham, a Preacher, in the Benton County Daily Record, on May 23, 2010.

"Who are the people promoting racist laws like what Arizona has just passed? Arizona now requires brown people to carry identification, or risk arrest. That's what the fascist, communist, apartheid, and totalitarian nations do - not Americans".

He cites Leviticus and other Bible verses to justify his stand in lashing out at Arizona for composing a law that is almost a replica of the Federal law. This is an example of a law that is not enforced by the Federal Government. Reverend Grisham says Jesus would not have been able to immigrate into Egypt and would have been killed by Herod. Then he parades out an illegal and portrays him as one who walks on water. However, since he is illegal, although the allegation is that he has lived here as a young tyke, he is now a criminal. Of course he should be given immunity (along with the rest of the illegal persons) and attend collage under the Dream Act, as a true guest of the taxpayers.

Lowell Grisham continues:

"That's a sane, humane, compelling change to our broken and abusive system of immigration laws. Yet the DREAM Act has failed in Congress since it was first introduced in 2001. Does anyone read their Bibles?"

Repeatedly the United States is demonized and chastised as a terrible bunch of people. Not only are we Americans providing free medical care to illegal aliens, but we are expected to provide free college education.

The border protection is a gigantic problem. A country is defined by its culture, language and borders. The powers to be in Washington are conducting an all out effort to promote open borders. President Obama, during a visit by the Mexican President, Felipe Calderon, declared the United States to be borderless. In essence, the United States does not exist as a nation. Now what? Felipe Calderon expressed his dismay over the Arizona law and any attempts or expressions to control the border. Again, President Obama, during the Calderon speech, acted subservient to the Mexican President. Apparently the citizens of the United States are on the wrong side of the border fence issue. Nationwide the taxpayers are expected to foot the bill for the vast educational and medical expenses of the illegal aliens. Such is the Dream Act.

Michael Savage pointed out that everyone subscribes for special treatment. They are all victims. This results in a gnawing problem of the multiples of individuals who claims special rights because they are victims. In New York City, a $3.2 million building was renovated for about one hundred gay students. It is called the Harvey Milk High School. This is yet another scam upon the taxpayer.

By 2003, the New York City school system could boast that 41 percent of its schools acquired a failing grade by the New York Department of Education.

One must be delusional if they cannot formulate a conclusion as to how disastrous the New York City school systems are. Yet, Ninga Segarra, the President of the New York City Board of Education and Mayor Michael Bloomberg continue on their merry way, spending with extravagance without any possibility of return. Something that would not be done if one was risking personal investment money.

How many dollars did the NEA contribute to the Democrats? Is it in the hundreds of millions? These are originally tax dollars. How else could they acquire the money?

Standardizing education at the federal level is a disaster. For example:

1. Text books are being rewritten to promote an ultra liberal agenda.
2. Homosexuality is being promoted - like it is an alright life style.
3. Centralization of control removes critical element of state and local inputs.
4. Parental involvement will be further minimized. Control over curriculum is removed from the state and local people.
5. More dollars thrown at the problem will assist the teachers union; however, it will not increase educational levels. Government intermeddling in the educational system is consistent with failure. A change in direction cannot take place with these ridiculously funded programs, such as a race to the top. Standards are falling and more than a proportionate number of students are failing. This is hap-

pening despite the vast increases in funding. From a political stand-point, the good sound bite is captivating. The lock step thinkers are enthused. By all reasonable measurements our geniuses are falling behind even third world countries. The detrimental effect in compet-ing on a global scale is incalculable. The teachers unions have been provided, by taxpayers, their own bailout plans. In the 2010 budget 41 billion dollars is programmed for the teachers union. The states are unable or unwilling to use their revenue for this purpose. Califor-nia received billions of these federal tax dollars. Yet they are bank-rupt and the responsibility goes unmet as the state has terminated teachers. What happened to the money?

Now at the national level, the teachers unions, true to form, are request-ing additional funding in the amount of 26 billion dollars. If these funds are not forthcoming, the threat is that there will be a layoff or suspension of 300,000 teachers. We are further told of the negative effect on our children and the future inability to take their competitive place in the world. The promulgators of this façade do not let it be known that the funds are for the teacher's retirement plans. In California the aggregate retirement plans garner 60 percent of the states entire budget for pension funds. Obviously, along with numerous other plans and programs, it is simply not sustainable.

6. A vested interest in formulating a hypothesis to even solve segments of a problem is obliterated. The current scale of operations does not consider solving a problem. It is being designed along deleterious government thought, resulting in curtailing educational progress.

So while Washington explores yet another concocted scheme, our pupils fall further behind and the teachers along with their unions prosper.

By March 2010, the government took over the student loans. Here again we deal this outright lies as the government grasps more power. This one in concert and an integral part of the health care bill. It does not produce a sur-plus. Here we have another inversion where a surplus is actually a sizeable deficit. The cost, similar to the health care bill, is incalculable. However, the student loan takeover is not without its merits. If one went to work for the government for a period of at least ten years, the debt would be forgiven. Now another program or method to gather people into government jobs and away from the private sector is being developed. Also, and importantly, government exercises its control by getting to determine who should get the loans.

Education is being taken from the domain of the states and transplanted into centralized government. States are continually unable to reach the vast and increasing costs of educational funding. Union wages are out of hand. Apparently, there is only one state fighting these constant increases, and that is New Jersey.

In August of 2010, Congress did grant $ 26 billion dollars to the teacher's pension funds. Herein are more deficit expenditures for the benefit of the teachers union. At the time of the passage of the bill, the amount of jobs saved was said to be 106,000. Again, we can observe another fabrication.

Many of these programs are promoted as a pay as you go situation. Often it is covering the costs by increases in specific taxes, especially corporations. Recently the statement was made as to a tax on entities doing business outside the U.S.

Education is rapidly being centralized into federal government system of control.

CHAPTER 5

PROMOTION OF
HATRED AND RACISISM

There is a grasp at accusing America of apartheid,

Immediately after the passage of the bill health care bill, the Democrats embarked upon a plan to entrench themselves behind the legislation by attacking those against the bill. Carefully selected was the Tea Party movement, which was engaged at this specific time in a minor meeting or demonstration in Washington D.C. In an attempt to provoke the Tea Party, four members of Congress, with accompanying cameras, strolled through the crowd. It was a crude attempt at provocation. When they failed to elicit a negative response, they concocted a story of being verbally attacked by racial and homophobic slurs, and yes, one, Emanuel Cleaver of Kansas City, was alleged to have been spat upon. Congressman Lewis of Atlanta, Georgia, a primary leader in Civil Rights, lent himself to this unexplainable and indefensible behavior. Many members of the press, such as Cynthia Tucker, formally of the Atlanta Constitution, couldn't wait to excoriate the Tea Party movement for their racists and homophobic remarks and portray Lewis as a victim.

In an article entitled "The spit is unimportant, but what it represents is dangerous"? This was authored by Emanuel Cleaver and printed in the Kansas City Star. Here is something that did not happen extrapolated into something unimportant. Then he tells us what is important.

"The incident was trivial: the anger it represents is not. These are trying and serious times and call for thoughtful and serious people of all political persuasions to build our national community rather than tear it apart".

"Republican members ought to stop accusing Democrats and the president of laying the foundation for a socialist takeover. That is not true and they know it"

Well, Emanuel Cleaver should be able to recognize a foundation for socialism or in the alternative, Marxism. How can these programs designed to cripple the United States not have a high degree of credibility?

It (racism) all took a giant step forward when the NAACP decried the Tea Party people as racist. The racist weapon is wearing out. The users of the racist card have wrongly determined that it will have a positive happening or desired outcome concomitant with their point of view. It is worn out and is void, for the most part of keeping people, quiet - the shut up method. Instead of being placed on the defensive, people are rapidly taking offence to the phrase. The problem is that such overt actions create racism. That appears be the desired result. It promoted diversity to the detriment of unity. Quite the opposite is apparent. The pendulum that swings from the demonized capitalists to socialism can readily swing to communism.

The Russian newspaper, Pravda, in its editorials believes the United States is on their way to becoming a communist state.

Leonard Zeskind, in unison with the propagandists, composed his hateful rhetoric toward the Tea Party. This also was published in the Kansas City Star.

"Where does the anger come from to call congressmen hateful names?"

"The answer resides inside the tea party anthem-oft-repeated since the protests on Capitol Hill last September - 'to take Our Country Back'. Many fear that they have lost the country that was bequeathed to them-and to them alone-like an old pocket watch from their grandfather."

This is an absurd analogy. The tea party directs its energies toward debate and the inherent issues therein. This scares many in the establishment, because they cannot control their thoughts and expressions. Therefore they feel compelled to demonize them, while at the same time accuse them of being racist (among other things).

For example, as outlined by the author and columnist, Leonard Zeskind:

"The conservative Republicans operatives, who train these new actives, become the foot soldiers for the party's election campaigns."

"The hard core white nationalists who join the tea party movement hope to convert its implicit whiteness into an explicit and coherent racism".

"The old-line segregationist's lists who regard every piece of federal civil rights law as an abrogation of states rights."

Nowhere is this apparent in any of the Tea Party demonstrations or statements. They do not claim to be Republican, nor do they align themselves with the Republican Party. This is a group with many members and it is growing at an increasing rate. Thus, we have another giant sized lie by an apparent lock stepper.

Also joining this crowd in Washington D.C., to no doubt cause trouble, was Nancy Pelosi.

A talk show host, (Andrew Breitbart) personally stated that he would pay ten thousand dollars upon proof of the incident, to John Lewis. With all of the cameras, people and cell phones on the block, certainly someone could verify the historic event.

The Democrats, undeterred by their failed attempt to promote racism in the nation's capitol incident, awaited their chance at the NAACP convention in Kansas City. Indeed this turned out to be a summer event like no other. It accused the Tea Party of being racist and insisted that the situation be corrected.

Apparently, The Tea Party Express (a part of the organization) was eliminated from the Tea Party. From the outside the attack appears as successful.

Another bazaar situation followed the NAACP Convention. The incident vividly pointed out the perils and absurdity of political correctness. Andrew Breitbart, described as a media entrepreneur, released or caused to be released, an edited video which purported to contain racist remarks made by an official within the Department of Agriculture, Shirley Sherrod. The remarks dated back to a speech before the NAACP in March of 2010. The incident mentioned in the speech dates back a number of years when she was helping black farmers in Georgia. Apparently, she was not politically correct in that she failed to help a white farmer. In short, it turns out, as the white farmer stated, that Shirley Sherrod did help him. Suddenly, the FOX talk show host, Glen Beck, was dragged into the fray as the person who was to divulge the remark as racist. The tall tale was enough to invoke political correctness and fire the official. The Department of Agriculture, later, after political embarrassment, recanted and offered reinstatement or another position.

CNN gutted other news for days to make this a fast breaking news story, propelling Sherrod to instant stardom. The video tape was played in its entirety. The accolades came from all directions. Apparently, the racist remarks were taken out of context and placed into the proper framework by playing this entire tape. It appears as a sizeable setup. Many questions are raised by this saga. We did not hear of her qualifications and what she actually did to help farmers. How many of the farmers were white?

Sherrod has a penchant for diversity. Specifically, she proclaimed a favorable inclination toward "poor" people and against "rich" people. This is not deductive reasoning, but is taken from the words contained in playing the video. Maybe she is a good person doing a fine job. It's just that the circumstances look faulty.

Shortly thereafter the Washington D.C. incident, to formulate a continuum, with the racists and violence programs, and the accusing thereof, Representative Clairbourne accused the Republicans of promoting violence against Democrats. Yet there was a failure to report the threats and assertive violent actions against Republicans. This program of accusing the opponents was well developed before the signing of the Health Care Bill. Specifically, Dennis Moore, a Democrat representing Kansas City, Kansas, stated that he was threatened. Incidentally he cited personal reasons as to why he is not going to run for reelection in his district. Guess why?

Right wing talk show hosts are accused of fostering violence by their rhetoric. Yet, the left wing radical networks (Air American and Move On. Org.) had individuals calling for the assassination of George W. Bush.

CHAPTER 6

DISINFORMATION MORE TAXES ECONOMIC SETBACKS

Many are finally, after being in office for over a year, questioning the motives of President Obama. There is a lot of speculation on this matter. Logically, it appears as unmistakable, that he subscribes to the destruction of our country.

Obama made the statement that now is not the time for profits. They will come later. Is this not words of a dictator? Here is a president determining a corporate profit structure. This really invites investment culminating in jobs.

The convoluted and controlled press, if one is to believe the poll numbers, has apparently not been effective is swaying public opinion. The vast majority of citizens oppose the legislation and encompassing federal regulations.

President Obama constantly circumvents answers to questions by stating, "This is area where there has been a whole lot of misinformation."

This element of misinformation was not part of a response to be emanated from an attendee who inquired, in a town hall meeting, as to the thought process of initiating more taxes with the health bill when we are already over taxed. Obviously, the President would not dare to give her a straight answer.

According to the insightful research of Senator John Thune, the Obama, Reid, and Pelosi health care bill contains a massive 569. billion dollar tax increase. Over 60 billion in new taxes will be collected before any benefits can be derived from the medical system. The recipients will have to wait until 2014.

Here is a slight inward look at the anomaly:

1. Taxes on the persons unable to afford insurance or fail to purchase insurance.
2. A middle-class tax on Americans via the excise tax on existing health insurance plans.
3. Tax on hiring. This is in addition to those unemployed persons for whom the employer must support.
4. To slow down economic growth, there are additional taxes on investment income.
5. Tax plus fees on medical devices that will have to be paid by the patient. Here is another example of cost additions being attached to the Obama, Reid and Pelosi health care bill.
6. The taxes that go into effect with this scheme are not adjusted for inflation. Thus, as with the Alternative Minimum Tax, it will encompass a vest segment of the society. At the onset, it appears to only affect the high income people.

Certainly this list is not all inclusive. It does portray the medical bill as being designed for tax collections, and not medical care. Perhaps one can view the medical systems as incidental.

Paperwork proliferation will have a devastating effect on business. It is debilitating enough without all of this legislation and subsequent regulation. For example the enormity of the health care bill requires businesses to file a tax form for all vendors that sell business $600. or more in a given year. Obviously, this paper work nightmare does not have anything reasonable approaching the Health Care Bill. Already a form has to be submitted for payments to contractual individuals who reach $600. Somehow, failure to inculcate this into the system will result in a loss of $19 billion in tax revenue. This within itself is not discernable. On the other side of the ledger, more people will have to be hired by the IRS to process the paperwork. Here we have a typical process of more government employees equaling a corresponding increase in the private sector burden.

Again, we must note the crippling of private sector jobs as a result of decreasing profits that could be reinvested in the business. When an economy arrives at a point to where the government is smothering the private sector, it can be expected that employment will contract exponentially.

These legislature and executive actions are obviously, ill advised-recurring refrains. The big budget will be borne by the future generations. How could they possibly pay even part of this astronomical amount of money?

Billions of the tax dollars are missing. The government is inveterate in its quest of finding ways of spending more money. There is just a handout program without a control system. Although, one cannot determine the use of the funds, a reasonable and prudent person can easily conclude that it is void of positive effects.

Other elements are also at work. Taxes are going to be raised on the population. The rich are expected to pay even more in taxes. This is a prime example of the divisions leading to class warfare. There are the clean air laws that are just waiting to be enacted. Can one imagine a tax on air like carbon dioxide? Is this not one of the giant size hoaxes perpetrated on practically all of the world wide populations, which will exclude the real polluters like India and China?

CHAPTER 7

ENVIRONMENT

Climate change is a giant hoax, which lacks scientific proof. To make their case, the environmentalists release what they claim to be scientific truths. Others are manipulated into believing that the earth is experiencing a global warming trend. However, they possess the intelligence to inquire that if indeed this is true, how could mankind be responsible for the occurrence and how could we act to change it?

Newsworthy items can be used to further the claim of global warming. Among the examples is Dengue fever. Although there is not a scintilla of evidence, the statement was made that the emergence of Dengue fever into the United States was occurring as a result of global warming. The same environmental problem was attributed to terrible fires in California. Allegedly, scientists agreed that a one degree increase in temperature caused the fires - a Sixty Minutes fairytale by Scott Pulley.

Now we have big chunks of icebergs breaking loose in Greenland. The threats to the polar bears are constantly increasing. Scientists are going into the habitat and measuring the size of the polar bears, like this portend their extinction. Yet, we are deprived of the news of the polar bear population increased from approximately 5000 to 25000 since the 1950s. Void of scientific evidence, the powers who usurped authority, express as fact, and the planet is experiencing warming caused by carbon and that "man" is the cause of this problem. Further, that the disaster is rapidly getting worse and we must act immediately -while we still have the chance. For the secular progressives, urgency is a key word.

One, Carol Mehl, writing an editorial in the Kansas City Star (August 18, 2010), meticulously alluded to the main points set forth by those claiming to be global climatologists.

"Quality of life on Earth hangs in the balance, and the United States has yet to step up to the plate in legislation aimed at the reduction of this nation's carbon emitted by the use of fossil fuels. Cap-and-trade legislation or carbon tax legislation would meaningfully point us toward sustainable energy production."
"There are those who disbelieve that the Earth is warming and that humans have caused it even though the most credible scientists concur in this conclusion."

Who are these credible scientists? No one has offered up the evidence that fossil fuel emissions have any effect on the global warming. In fact nowhere has a hypothesis been successfully tested that reached the conclusion that humans have caused changes in the environment. Yet these people are ready to sell and tax corporations on their carbon emissions. The tax has to be passed on to the citizens. Thus, we will have another tax to pay, making energy even more expensive.

In the midst of all of these environmental happenings, ethanol and its massive subsidies come to mind. It is unfortunately projected to offset the alleged environmental mishaps of oil pollution. All of this translates into big power for the politicians.
Charles Goyette, The Dollar Meltdown, cites the Economist (Dec.2007):

"There are two hundred different government subsidies in the ethanol program, requiring taxpayers to fork over a whopping $1.90 per gallon to producers."

Ethanol is central to the discussion. It crosses lines from agricultural payouts, to refinement as an efficient fuel, to decreasing the food supply. Corn is a necessary food. A shortage of supply of corn can cause food riots in rice. Imagined shortages in corn has already caused near riots in rice in the Philippines. California, when it appeared that a shortage of rice was a possibility, limited purchases of this food staple. Increases in the cost of food can start riots. People need sustenance and must have the resources to pay for it. Corn is used for animal feed. Consequently, shortages of corn can cause a steep rise in beef prices. Interference by the politically inspired subsidies can extend to a number of negative causes. The resulting problems become inexorable. Somehow they are mentally isolated from the consequences. Corn syrup is a poison in its own right. It is one of the contributed factors to obesity. The liver cannot properly process corn syrup. It turns into fat. The Department of Agriculture has heavily subsidized programs. Corn syrup is one of them. It is a cheap product, which is allowed to be sold, without even a warning. As an additional note, aspartame, the artificial sweetener, turns out to be poisonous. Somehow, Congress legalized its sale. The derivative of corn is corn syrup. Somehow, it is to appear on food labels as something else, perhaps fructose. This will decrease consumer awareness of the corn syrup in their supermarket purchases. Where is the FDA on this one?

The cost to the taxpayer for a gallon of ethanol far exceeds the cost of oil. It is less efficient and therefore yields less miles per gallon. The use of energy to produce ethanol is 130 % greater than its yield. Additionally, the ordinary engine is not made to burn ethanol, yet it placed in the supply chain, where a free choice is not being considered.

To attempt to dramatize the need to respond to climate change, the global planners had to have a giant sized get together. Copenhagen was selected for the meeting. Ironically, Copenhagen had a major snow storm. Logical feasibility was sadly lacking. If the objective of the meeting was to involve the world into promoting such a program, it failed miserably. Secretary of State Hillary Clinton was fairly much exposed on the foolishness of this endeavor. She pledged billions of dollars to fight global warming. The only thing it would provide is U.S. taxpayer's money for the Dictators of the world. These attendees are the same people who applaud hate speakers, such as Hugo Chavez, especially when it is targeting the United States. Hillary Clinton was also instrumental in supplying a billion dollars to Hamas. This was under the guise of helping the people of Gaza. The interests of peace, in the Middle East, are not being well served.

In essence the developed countries must ante up vast sums to assist developing nations to reduce their future emissions. The proposition is that the underdeveloped nations of the world will, after they siphon off considerable sums of money, build cleaner coal fired facilities and nuclear plants. Judging from the past, it will never happen. These governments are characterized by corruption. President Obama made a pretense of promoting energy security. He alluded to promoting nuclear energy. Obama mentions one plant, which will probably not come on line for ten years, as a miraculous accomplishment. Why is the President not called to task on this issue? This country should be building numerous nuclear plants, instead of miring in inhibiting events of the past. The technology for the production and safety of nuclear energy has vastly improved, over the years. These technological progressions should be recognized as a signal to vigorously pursue expansion of the industry, and the development of private sector jobs, which could be involved in this process. Many of these jobs would be unionized. Here is another illustration of an Administration stopping the job creating mechanisms.

China and India need to do something positive about their pollution. These nations however, are not allowing themselves to be placed in a defenseless environmental corner. The promoters of this global warming hoax insinuate that the United States and other developing countries like China and India are causing the toxic gases that are responsible for global warming. They always offer up causal evidence as if it is proof of impending crises that threatens all of mankind and therefore requires a coordinated response. Some of the speech encompasses "green jobs". Here we are confronted by an economic dilemma which is gyrating toward a depression with uncontrollable inflation and the powers to be are talking about creating a few government funded jobs. The private enterprises that could be instrumental in generating technological advances and production of future energy systems are currently unmotivated or financially inhibited. The primary reason is the negative effect created by government and its programs that create or attack the private side of the economy. Not just another demoralizing statement.

Note that nanotechnology is not coming out of the so called woodwork to promote our well being.

Politicians, regardless of being a Democrat or Republican, gyrate toward the workings of government. If government can be perceived as the sole entity to assist society in their dilemmas, they must administer the solutions, even though it leads to the vilification of the capitalistic private enterprise. Laws and regulations (not interchangeable) are formulated by the government agencies. Many firms will have folded up. Free market initiatives are being depleted.

CHAPTER 8

FINANCE ECONOMICS REGULATIONS

Often we hear that there is enough blame to go around. These bromides serve, to some extent, the indistinguishable elements where confusion can be added to the inexorable problem. There has to be a compelling urge to simplify the matters and break through the lies and double talk. Many factors need to be mentioned.

There was a failure of regulations, particularly financial institutions. Actually, regulations from the 1930s were in place to protect the economy from the excessive greed of certain capitalists and the corruptness of the lobbyists and elected officials. Bank and brokerage houses were separate entities (Glass Stegal Act). Insurance companies had restrictions on the type of investments they could make. Regulatory agencies monitored the behavior of the financial institutions, at least some of us thought.

The Community Reinvestment Act was signed into law by Jimmy Carter in 1977. Banks as a result of this Act were forced to provide loans to business, homeowners and potential homeowners with abysmal credit. Then came Government, along with its conspirators, to compromise and eventually destroy the free market system. First viable regulations were eliminated. In a stair step approach, after this played itself out, more existing regulations were, metaphorically speaking, thrown out the window. This non enforcement provided the motivation to operate outside a lawful system. The prime example Banks were forced to make real estate loans to unqualified persons and send them to a sort of a quasi government agency - Freddie Mac and Fannie Mae. The building and construction industry, in the short run, with the use of illegal labor, prospered. Thus began the prime loan mess, which as we know culminated in the demise of our economy. The diabolical consequences of the reverses in the housing industry moved world wide. International banks taking on this bad (now called toxic) debt were severely mired in a rapidly dissolving system. The gambling tools, derivatives of a zero sum nature, totals in the trillions of dollars. Thanks to Congress and its open pocketbook policies, Freddie Mac and Fannie May are permanent "wards" of the state. Their "top" executives receive millions of dollars in bonuses. This is a totally inept government organization.

The American consumer is paramount in our capitalistic economy. The reality of the economy conditions was brought into the mindset of the consuming public. Many were unable to make their credit card or house payments. Facing mounting debt and an inability to pay even the minimum requirements, many Americans became desperate and stopped spending. Discretionary income became scarce. Decreases in private sector expenditures, have had a negative ripple effect on the economy, and is a major contributing factor to galloping unemployment.

Wall Street was involved in brokering these pathetic mortgages to unsuspecting investors. Coupled with other activities, such as hedging and over leveraging, gyrated the investment institutions into paralysis.

The G20 meetings in London culminated in emphasizing the world wide contamination. The World Bank and International Monetary fund will receive funds that may have as one of its goals to cover up the complexity and magnitude of this inexorable problem. The International Monetary Fund alone will receive over a trillion dollars, the vast majority of this coming from the US. This is money the country does not have. The United Nations, one of our enemies, has set forth a supposition, despite our world wide contributions to dismal societies, that the United States is a cheap nation. Nowhere has any country come close to the generosity of the United States. One has to wonder how long this propaganda can continues. Also, we have ex presidents (Jimmy Carter and Billy Clinton) that visit the world and call this country stingy - among other things.

The London G20 meeting has attendees who can be viewed as enemies of the United States. Others are on the periphery of undermining the United States. Not withstanding that we as Americans are expected to ante up the cash to bail out the world after being blamed for the tragedy.

Some countries do have valid concerns. China for example is concentrating on the safety of the trillion dollars they hold in U.S. Treasury Bonds and Notes. Germany, Austria and other Western European Countries have deep loans to the former East block countries, e.g., Poland, Hungary, and

Romania. These countries borrowed heavily. The deflation of their currency, in comparison to the Euro, resulted in these countries, not being able to pay on the debt. Those entities loaning the money have steadfastly refused to bail them out. Should they be bailed out? That is a case for discussion. However, is it a responsibility of the United States to pay for a bailout? What are the parameters of the United States in conjunction to other countries in the foreign bailout program? How many financial elements will we ante up to before we are actually suffering from bankruptcy? One must be careful to note the inflationary damage. Zimbabwe is not a remote memory. Other countries will suffer a worse fate (if that is possible).

The G-20 meeting in October 2010 was the most chaotic of any of the gatherings. It was actually a harbinger of the currency wars. A few of the participants, in order to improve their export markets, threatened to devalue their currency. The dollar is too weak to achieve the necessary influence. Reliance is now on the International Monetary Fund and the World Bank to attempt stability. The further demise of the dollar is evident. By November 2010, again a G20 meeting, this time in Korea, glaringly showed the U.S. in a particularly negative situation. Prior to the meeting, China had their diplomats circle the wagons around the world. The goal was to convince them to influence the U.S. to not devalue the dollar. Here we are expressing the inadequate approach of China's trading policy in not upgrading the Yuan to supposedly reflect a more accurate foreign exchange.

Obama during his expensive visit to Asia continually talked about "jobs" for the U.S. This was to play for the American audience. It did not gain much attention from the Asians. No matter how many times he mentioned it, the message failed. Repetition does not make the statement true. A conclusion is to relegate the utterance to propaganda. The question is how many jobs were lost to Asia- not gained. Korea was an example of failed attempts. Korea sells into the U.S. market. Yet American cannot gain entrance into the South Korean market. It is off limits. Any efforts to change the situation and bring down the trade barriers have gone for naught.

After the G-20 meeting, the attendees seemed to go their separate ways. Coordinated efforts are seemingly a past tense. Without U.S. leadership, continued currency warfare is more of likelihood.

China is concerned about the diminishment of the dollar, secondary to the policy of the Federal Reserve's resolve to go ahead and create money by running the printing presses. The excuse used is to stimulate the economy by flooding money into the banks. The financial institutions, in turn, will have loan able funds. Two items of note:

1. The banks already have ample funds to make loans.
2. Very few entities or individuals are borrowing.
3. This has been tried before, by none other than the Obama administration. It failed miserably.

The world is awash with dictators. The world is void of much needed leadership. The environment is a further distraction for economic development. There are numerous speeches by President Obama for the development of programs for energy independence. Yet the opposite is true.

Sabotaged by the following:

1. Useless government spending on windmills
2. Prohibit drilling by oil companies and digging for coal
3. Restrict permits for nuclear plants
4. Close out programs for the storing of nuclear waste - as in Nevada
5. Ruthlessly tax the energy producers
6. Constant propaganda that thrives on misconceptions and outright lies, e.g., save money, create jobs (green jobs), create energy efficiency, secure energy independence, jump start the economy, slash carbon emissions to give us a better life
7. Cajole investments by inefficient firms into the renewable energy enigma by providing tax incentives, thereby taking resources from an efficient element of private resource.
8. Fail on purpose in areas that are developed into crises situations, such as the Gulf Oil Spill and Katrina.
9. There are not any contingency plans.

Obama does not have an energy plan. Every time we hear of someone raving about making progress in the renewable energy area, for example, windmills as a new technology, replacing traditional electrical output, a sizeable taxpayer subsidy is involved. It cannot stand on its own merits, nor could renewable energy make a sizeable dent in energy needs. The theme among the lock steppers is echoed in repeated loud tones. It emphasizes creating a system, which will make us energy independent, particularly from having to import oil from the Middle East. Yet at every turn, involved in the development of the domestic oil industry, the U.S. has large obstacles placed in its path by none other than the Obama administration.

The United Nations sponsored Copenhagen conference wherein members of a plethora of countries met in December 2009, fast became a circus that lacked any humor or entertainment value. Yet it inspired many to show how they march in lock step.

Here are cites of the lock step march toward convincing us that we are in peril. This one entitled "U.S. must lead the way in reducing Carbon." Reference taken from, the December 5th issue of the Kansas City Star.

"So it will take cool-headed thinking by political leaders to establish meaningful programs to contend with man-made global warming. (Yes-for all the strident skeptics out there-science clearly shows the Earth is getting warmer and yes, it's partly because of greenhouse gas emissions.)."

The strident skeptics are called doubters by Al Gore. What science are they talking about? Nowhere, has a hypothesis been proven, by anyone, (not even a scientist) to state that we indeed have global warming. Even if we did have global warming, how would humans be the cause for warming the planet?

To further quote this article:

"Developed nations that currently spew the most harmful emissions- led by the United States, and including Germany, Britain, France and Australia - should agree to even more robust cuts in future carbon emissions."

Where is China and India in all of these carbon footprints?
To continue:

"This is no time for timidity. While President Barrack Obama deserves much credit for dumping the head-in-the-sand approach of former President George W. Bush on this issue, Osama's recently proposed carbon emissions reduction plan is nowhere as drastic as needed. He should announce a bolder initiative and then work with congress to approve it in 2010."

Before the end of this distorted conference, Hillary Clinton, our Secretary of State, pledged one hundred billion dollars toward this perverted planetary contrivance. This is money we do not have. And why not, in the blame game we are the cause of all of these so called world ills.

To continue once again:

"The developed countries must come forward with money to help the neediest developing nations reduce their future emissions. Those funds can be used to build cleaner coal-fired plants, for instance, and nuclear-powered facilities."

Isn't this what we need to build for our economic and security well being? Is it not a fact that Obama administration prohibits us from doing this? Yet it is a solution for the needy countries.

To once again continue:

"All the countries should agree to aggressively cut the use of fossil fuels (especially coal and oil) and to improve energy efficiency."
"Steps include more reliance on renewable energy, such as cleaner wind and solar sources; which deserve government encouragement and subsidies. Tougher auto efficiency requirements are needed not just in the U.S. but also China, India and other developing countries".
"The Copenhagen conference will be a huge victory if it demonstrates that dealing with global warming has become a true partnership among the nations of the world."

Can you imaging have a partnership among this group. Hugo Chaves, Obama's dictator friend from Venezuela, lambasted Capitalism (and Obama). This aspect can be expected. However, the Copenhagen audience was enthusiastically applauding Hugo and showing their distain and hatred for the United States. The Zimbabwe dictator also received a warm welcome from the Copenhagen gathering. Was this an example of a typical United Nations gathering?

These people are well organized and feverously press their agenda to steal the wealth of the United States. This is not an element of paranoia. Just examine the actions of practically all of these nations, which, in one example, are directed toward using global warming as a tool to extract an extravagant amount of money for their own dictatorships. They are further emboldened by an administration that continuously undermines and blames the U.S. for all of the world ills. Hillary Clinton, our esteemed Secretary of State, laid the blame on us for enhancing the narcotics activity in Mexico. Indeed, it was our fault because we purchase drugs. Hey, peek at this example, what about the illegal aliens who buy the drugs. How many million are there of those?

The article further accuses the U.S. of having caused global warming for years. Hey, what about the years we freeze to death? Don't they count? Maybe that is why the term climate change is used in lieu of global warming.

Business Obstacles: (minimizing motivations for investment)

Here we have the Lilly Ledbetter Act, legally known as the Fair Play Act. How fair is it for firms to be sued by someone claiming to be a victim of wage discrimination? The actions could have taken place a number of years ago. The Fair Play Act can survive the Statute Of Limitations by extending litigation in perpetuity. This is a gigantic political gift to the Trial Lawyers. Businesses will have a continuous legal threat. How can a defense be formulated after a period, of say, ten years? Many documents will have been dispensed to the trash heap. Perhaps many of the employee witnesses will have moved to other pastures. In maintaining an action, past agreements will be invalidated and the firm will acquire a sizeable burden of proof. This was among the first of the executive triumphs of the Obama Administration. It serves as a forerunner of other plans and programs designed to inhibit the constituency.

Despite the economic devastation, the perpetrators are still on the march, creating yet more wreckage. Nowhere is their positive statement pertaining to the free market place. It is government that must save the day. Ironically the powers are busy selling and performing the same methodologies. The programs that failed us miserably in the past are destined to destroy us American people in the future.

Keynesian economics draws immense attention when it is expedient to mention something that generates a degree of sophisticated economic knowledge. To a mildly trained brain, it depicts a lack of understanding. It shows us as, a subterfuge that is purposely designed to convince a population that proper actions are taking place.

John Maynard Keynes did not diminish private capital spending. Government in growth times (economic expansion) should have revenue surpluses to set aside for the recessionary periods. The economic times of contraction would experience government expanding the money supply to offset the negative effects and thereby assist the economy. In reality, as we are aware, the government accelerates its spending, regardless of economic conditions. Then when it spends, in recessionary periods, it proclaims its Keynesian prerogatives.

Continuing with the Keynesian didactics, the free market place determines the rate of interest and the marginal efficiency of capital. A marginally astute business person will not be inclined to borrow money for investment when the cost of renting capital (interest) is more than what is the projected return. A business would borrow money at the market rate of interest, after determining it would experience a return on the use of money. The U.S. Government, in an effort to generate economic activity, reduced the interest rate to zero. It failed to influence private sector borrowing. Zero interest rates have been used by the Japanese for an extensive period of time; essentially starting in the late 1980s.This is coincidently the time frame when the Japanese economy and stock market started its tumble. Many of those who borrow are unable to repay the loans, even at the zero rates. The zero rates are an encouragement to borrow. Economically it is unrealistic to create such a circumstance.

The inadequacy of government is pointed out by the lack of success of the 700 billion TARP program. The bail out plan is void of a strategy, and as such is doomed to failure. The vital elements for success are tragically missing. The program was contrived to provide the wrecking ball to the economy and leave close to a majority of the private sector citizens exposed to unemployment. The taxpayers have been denied an accounting of the use of the funds. Has the TARP money been stolen? Many of the Banks who were forced to take TARP money are returning it as fast as possible in a desperate effort to avoid the drastic government controls. This was set up as a slush fund with specific earmarks. Why are these funds not returned to the taxpayers?

Under the guise of energy independence and in addition to ameliorating our escalating imports the Obama administration has essentially halted drilling for oil, digging for coal and building nuclear plants. How perverse?

The recently developing policies are directed in many areas. A common thread exists, which is to deprive the citizen of his or her freedoms. The vital liberty of private property is under assault. The Government has undertaken a decisive plan to redistribute the wealth. This is an admitted fact by the Obama administration. Specifically, many bureaucracies are being created to formulate a multitude of elements to transfer wealth (to the Government) and develop enormous control over the population.

1. Ridiculous Environmental controls
2. Takeover of medical care
3. Unjust taxes resulting in confiscation

The enormity of the problem cannot be understated. It is uncompromising. They have acquired the political power to destroy us by many means, one of which is bankruptcy. Remember that the Glorious Revolution, French Revolution and the Russian Revolution grew out of bankruptcy. This is a fair sized warning. It could happen here. Something enormously negative is bound to happen.

JUSTICE:

A glance of the Department of Justice, illustrates how it is in lock step with the Obama Administration. The Department is rapidly streaking toward the radical left. At least nine lawyers recently hired raised numerous eyebrows when it was discovered that they had the common denominator of having represented detainees of Guantanamo. The move was ostentatious. Criticism of this packing the Department of Justice brought about outrageous attacks by the leftists. Yet these appointments take place at a time the United States is at war.

If the courts rule against the administrations wishes, then the regulators take over. The same result is happening in the interpretation of the legislature. Only this takes on an additional impetus, in that if Congress does not pass legislation, the regulatory agencies will proceed as if the legislation prescribed into the law.

Charles Krauthammer in his article, Who Makes the Laws, Anyway? Not Congress? The Kansas City Star, August 10, 2010, elaborated on this specific issue.

"A draft memo surfaced from the Homeland Security Department suggesting ways to circumvent existing law to allow several categories of illegal immigrants to avoid deportation and. indeed, for some to be granted permanent residency. Most disturbing was the stated rationale. This was proposed 'in the absence of Comprehensive Immigration Reform."

"This is not how a constitutional democracy should work. Administrators administrate the law, they don't change it. That's the legislator's job."

Continuing along the same line, but a different aspect of government control:

"A 2007 Supreme Court ruling gave the Environmental Protection Agency the authority to regulate carbon emissions if it could demonstrate that they threaten human health and the environment. The Obama EPA made the finding, granting itself a huge expansion of power and, noted The Washington Post, sending 'a message to Congress."
"It is not a terribly subtle message: Enact cap-and-trade legislation-taxing and heavily regulating carbon-based energy-or the EPA will do so unilaterally. As Frank O'Donnell of Clean Air Watch noted, such a finding 'is likely to help light a fire under the Congress to get it moving."

The Supreme Court, perhaps unwittingly, provided a loop hole for the EPA, to assert its authority, by making such a profound and unproven scientific finding that carbon emissions are harmful. Perhaps the Supreme Court did not anticipate that regulatory action and the grabbing of power by the Executive Branch. It ripped its ruling to shreds.

On the issue of abortion, did the Supreme Court consider as far back as 1973, in the Rowe B. Wade case, that the decision would set the stage for over fifty million abortions in the United States? In essence, this case created an entire industry. With taxpayers' funds, this trend has gone world wide.

The packing of the court is yet another methodology to promote the "taking over" of the free society. Upon the first vacancy, the expedient measures were put in place. Sotomayor was selected for the Bench. She was promoted as a Latina from an unprivileged broken family, who as a minority rose to scholarly levels and graduated from an Ivy League law school. Everything was right and resulted in a gratifying achievement. The problem is the agenda. While on the bench in New York City, she had too far many cases overturned by the Supreme Court. A clear warning sign came when her leftist press friends, mentioned in passing, that the cases were overturned on a technicality. During her Senate hearings for confirmation to the bench, Sotomayor was asked if she would uphold the constitutional amendment that guarantees the right to bear arms. She enthusiastically replied in the affirmative. Yet, among Sotomayor's initial Supreme Court cases, was the Chicago litigation on the right to bear arms. She promptly voted against such rights. Sotomayor was on the minority side of this important issue. However, it scraped by on 5 to 4 vote. The Constitution is clear on this matter. It states that a citizen has a right to bear arms. Yet, four members of the bench did not interpret the clearly worded document within its described prospective.

Saxby Chambliss, Republican Senator from Georgia, used straight forward reasoning in determining how he should vote.

"After reviewing the cases she decided, talking with lawyers who know her, and reviewing speeches and her testimony, I have concluded that I cannot support Judge Sotomayor's nomination. I am a strong supporter of the 2nd Amendment, and I am concerned about her reasoning in cases where she has considered this issue. I am concerned about her apparent leaning to use foreign law to interpret America's own laws and Constitution. Her lack of well-reasoned opinions is also troublesome."

The use of the interpretation of foreign law in relation to the U.S. Constitution and the inculcation of such statutes into our system is dangerous. It translates into a one world government, governed by the United Nations and maybe controlled by private international bankers. Incidentally the bureaucrats of the U.N. are the most highly paid.

Then came the next Supreme Court nominee, Elena Kagan, those entire background is ultra left. It is the perfect selection to pack the court for the leftist agenda. The left attempted to paint her as a moderate. Efforts were made to view her as not having judicial experience. It was a subterfuge. She is obviously not a moderate and prior judicial experience is not a factor of consideration. Her credentials as the Dean of Harvard Law School and other workings as Solicitor General offset her not sitting on a judicial bench. She was selected to replace the retiring Judge Stevens, who, although a left leaning member of the court was essentially moderate.

It was Obama, who alluded to Earl Warren as not being sufficiently liberal. Has his wish been fulfilled in Elena Kagan?

GUANTANAMO

Many of those released from the prison at Guantanamo Bay are back in action as leaders in various terrorist areas of the world, such as Somalia,

Yemen, and Afghanistan. Obama, in early 2010 decided not release from GITMO, some of the prisoners earlier selected to be sent to Yemen. What prompted this change of mind? Where will he now disperse these terrorists?

One such attack, written by columnist Eugene Robinson, was published in the Kansas City Star on March 14, 2010, lashed out at Liz Chaney, the daughter of Vice President Chaney.

The leftist portions of the press, when ever they feel threatened, gather their resources to undermine the criticizers and attempt to paint them as fanatics. Psychiatrist calls this projection.

Mr. Robinson alluded to Mc Carthyism as being a mild term to use for Liz Chaney. Sort of a quote - Liz Chaney had the gall to question the values of the new hires. The Supreme Court, Hamdan case is paraded out as a part of this response to Liz Chaney.

"Principal Deputy Solicitor General Neal, represented Osama bin Laden's driver, Salim Hamdan, in a case that went to the Supreme Court. In a 5-3 decision, the court sided with Hamdan and rules that the Bush Administration's military tribunals were unconstitutional."

Hamden was tried by a military tribunal. Eugene Robinson stated that the Supreme Court declared this military tribunal unconstitutional.

The article rattles on to suggest that Liz Chaney and her group, Keep America Safe, in their objections, prepare a denunciation of the federal judiciary.

To further quote:

"Or maybe what they really don't like is that pesky old Constitution with all its checks, balances and guarantees of due process. How inconvenient to live in a country that respects the rule of law."

He summarized the article declaring Liz Chaney's attacks as designed to wound President Obama politically. The article fails to mention, no less explain, why all of these lawyers happened to be hired. Instead it goes on to trump up inane (or at least not esoteric) statements questioning ones stance on the Supreme Court and the Constitution. Even superficial thinking could not lead one to deduct such absurdity by assigning a label of conflict of belief of the overall Constitution.

The group has subsequently been labeled, "the GITMO Bar Association". The people, who performed pro bono for the GITMO people, were appointed by the administration, essentially in masse. Isn't this matter of integrity? Many other good candidates could have been selected in lieu of choosing the "Gitmo bunch".

The question is not if the detainee terrorists can be entitled to a legal defense. Again the point is how all of a sudden these people are all appointed to Justice Department positions. What is the future agenda and how will they contribute to these programs? In other words, what is expected of them?

This article is important because it lays open the thinking and subsequent actions of the far left. Perhaps one could conclude that it places a spotlight on those who they most fear. One should examine the nature of the attacks on Sarah Palin.

LARGESSE

To undermine the Republicans, Carl Hiassen, writing the Miami Herald (March 20, 2010), titled, "Fantastic Plastic Shows GOP How to Party." It has as its objective to point out the out of control spending by Marco Rubio, the Republican candidate for the US Senate race in Florida.

"In fact, so many state GOP big-shots were living large off campaign donations that the party is now in manic damage-control mode."

Hiassen cites numerable exploitations of credit card use by the GOP. However, in this out of control system, there is no mention of the Democrats. This is a vital shortfall that shows the bias in reporting.

Nancy Pelosi has demanded and received her own US Air Force passenger plane for herself and her family. This is a separate creation of an elitist group. A very dangerous happening and alerts us to the grasp of power by an out of control member of the Congress.

Congressman Emanuel Cleaver leases a van that costs $2900. a month. His staffers cite other members of Congress who lease vehicles for almost as much. Simply, one extravagance does not justify another. The open pocket book of the taxpayer created this extreme, for which there is no discernable return.

Of course, there are many others, in both parties, doing more than just putting their hands in the till.

In some fashion the Savings and Loan debacle was a forerunner of the sub prime mortgages. It is a striking example of a lesson not learned. The sub prime menace is only one element of the crises. It is a global crisis. Government interventions have made it worse. Indeed, the future actions can only be projected to make it worse. The emphasis promulgates a transformation from a recession to a depression.

From the prospective of November 2008, Fannie Mae and Freddie Mac were too big to fail. Then there is City Group, which is too big to bail out. Bank America acquired two zombies, Country Wide Credit and Merrill Lynch. These are only examples. Lehman Brothers is a separate story. A few years back the Capital hedge fund needed to be bailed out. It was a separate, but noticeably pertinent, financial conundrum. At the nudging of the Federal Reserve, all of the big firms came to the rescue, except Lehman Brothers. As a consequence of their refraining from participating in the hedge fund bailout by the non public sector, Lehman fell through the bail out cracks in 2008. Lehman was in competition will other firms on Wall Street. Reports alluding to this selection process, to refrain Lehman from receiving bail out funds to diminish their competitiveness is just not believable.

Reflecting on history, a country does not exist that emanated from a government entity comprised primarily of Capitalism, which lapsed into socialism and continued its economic growth. Indeed, tragic results have followed, not only economically, but in loss of freedoms. Creeping socialism can lead to gigantic loss of freedoms. Among the last is the rights of free speech. All of a sudden, the government that people seek to protect it becomes an end within itself and extinguishes all resemblances of freedom. Remember the volunteers and brainwashed school children - they have their non thinking allegiances toward a radically prone government. By the time it becomes obvious the controlling measures of the government have solidified their unfavorable characteristics.

The underlying aspects of this government have created turmoil, finally, albeit all too late, became transparent to the masses. The analysis we hear about does not consider the three hundred trillion dollars in derivatives. These casino types of activities are world wide and are outside the realm of control.

Government spending drains resources from the private sector. Expansion of government increases government jobs and kills off private sector jobs. A mixed economy, Socialism or Marxism, siphons off the vitality needed to enhance private sector businesses. Government does not produce anything. Its primary basis is to interfere with the free market place and siphon off much of the indigenous wealth as possible, into its own treasury. On the other hand, private industry produces wealth. It is a system that increases standards of living. Socialism or Marxism serves to create a welfare state void of initiatives and innovations. Look at Russia. What innovations have they created? The Muslim culture has not had any innovations in hundreds of years.

The current system is so corrupt, that in order to be beneficial to society, the political system has to fail. This is in juxtaposition to the diabolical bailout program. Noticeably, it is tantamount to stealing the monies for the benefit of fraudulent characters, who masquerade those who are the sole persons to save the system. The three branches of Government are willing accomplices in this tragedy. When one looks at the gigantic bonuses, it becomes apparent that the citizen's power base has been decimated. As government continues to perceive itself as a needy entity, it will confiscate more funds and assets. These actions will drive more people into poverty. Through unemployment, taxes, and confiscation, the needy people in the population will grow. They recognize that running the printing presses is not sufficient.

Investments, as perceived by individuals, are not gambling. Monies allocated to retirement funds are expected to be readily available when needed. How can such expectations exist when fluctuations can vary by over fifty percent? Is this not gambling? The conventional wisdom is to dollar cost average or continues to fund the plan. In the long run the expectation is that a sizeable amount of wealth will be available for the golden years in life. This is also extended to the children of the family for education. When the time arrives for advanced studies, the preparation will provide its rewards in covering anticipated expenses. Really? Suppose the market is down. Will it recover in time to provide the needed monies?

Perhaps the supposition could be made that without stock market timing, it is gambling. What goes up must come down. But will it work in reverse? Previously, with rare exception it has. However, we are now in a totally unexplored area, which clouds the crystal ball. The investment world is complicated. Many so called experts have failed in the investment world.

Diversification is helpful in spreading the risks. However, it has its pitfalls. Caution is paramount. There are many areas of investments. It is essential to learn some of the many investment areas. This is in lieu of reliance on the so called experts.

Thomas Jefferson cited the problems of an unabated banking system.

"I believe banking institutions are now more dangerous to our liberties that standing armies. If the American people ever allow private banks to control the issue of their currency, first by inflation, then by deflation, the banks and corporations that will grow up around (the banks) will deprive the people of all property until their children wake up homeless on the continent their fathers conquered".

It appears as though massive manipulation is constantly taking place, not only in the stock market, but also with commodities and metals (particularly gold and silver). Central banks, at times, have difficulty in controlling gold. It inhibits their power. Therefore it is deemed necessary for them to manipulate the markets by leveraging (both long and short) and actually selling their inventory of gold. Over the summer of 2009 the International Monetary fund announces that it was going to sell one hundred billion in gold. Meanwhile China, Russia, India and other countries are buying gold.

China and Russia in particular are striving to change the reserve currency. The reserve currency is the US dollar. These countries realize that the dollar cannot sustain itself. The US, by its internal actions, is becoming a weaker nation. Printing of trillions of dollars in fiat currency is symptomatic of a nation unable or unwilling to provide for itself. A country as powerful as the United States is now gyrating toward eminent destruction.

Paul Krugman, in a New York Times article, pointed out the enigma of our Chinese problem in keeping the renminbi undervalued, which in turn provides for cheaper exports. How is the undervalued renminbi detrimental to our well being? Well, for one the currency manipulation saves us dollars in the market place in the purchase of Chinese exports. This drives up our import costs to the magnitude of creating massive balance of payments deficits. Our currency plies up in the form of a debt to foreign entities. A debtor nation may be forced into giving up elements of control. China holds close to 2 trillion of our dollars. This is used as a hatchet to inhibit actions to increase the value of the currency. Paul Krugman, is his own way, challenges the Treasury to respond to the Chinese and their "absurdity" of declaring that the renminbi is not undervalued. The case for the Treasury to act in concert with other elements of the government is impressive. He points out that if the Chinese dumped monetary assets, the value of the dollar would fall creating an environment for increasing exports and decreasing imports, which would be more expensive. China would lose on the decreased value of the dollar. The reckless increasing of the U.S. money supply is one of China's main concerns. Thus, the Chinese are seeking other methods to hedge their bets on the value of the dollar.

The Chinese may yield, from time to time, to slightly increase the value of the Juan. However, this will not extend to the desires of the Department of the Treasury. In fact attempting to have the Chinese increases the value of the Juan, will show the limited influence of Tim Geithner and the U.S. Treasury.

China has done a few things toward insuring their economic growth:

1. Diversify their dollar holdings into other currencies, particularly the EURO. Since then the EURO has had a precipitous decline in relation to other currencies.
2. Convert dollar holdings to gold.
3. Use credits and interchanges between other countries that are trading with China. In essence this will, in these specific instances, replace the dollars as a reserve currency. China, along with other countries is desirous of offsetting the dollar as a reserve currency. The suggestion is to develop a basket of currencies. If this became effective, it would be diminutive to the U.S. dollar. The consequences would be quite internally destructive. The decrease in the acceptance of the U.S. dollar will simultaneously increase inflation and decrease the standard of living. However, the basket of currencies will lose some of their purchasing power. The International Monetary Fund is more likely to replace the dollar with a created IMF currency. For this to happen, the U.S. will have to have demands on the dollar to such a magnitude that they will have no choice but to default. A gigantic debt, coupled with the inability to acquire more of its citizen's wealth, would be the factors that propel the nation into default. Actually, the wealth would be exhausted.

In further introspection, the outlook for China to change its position and increase the value of the Yuan is negligible. The U.S. does not press issues which are beneficial to it against a foreign sovereign. Not only did China escape conversation without having to change its currency, but it has been inversely rewarded with a prominent position in the World Bank, where it will be able to oversee and have inputs into its expenditures of American money. The main countries, in the World Bank decision making processes, are the United States, European Nations, Japan and now China.

Comparison of the United States and China must take into consideration the difference between the average wages of the workers. In the U.S.
average is $ 46381 per year. Per year, the Chinese worker averages $ 5667.
The Chinese are in a much weakened position than they would like to let the
outside world know. The Chinese consumption of goods and services are
not sufficient to sustain even the current standard of living. Many are leaving urban areas and returning to rural areas. Without exports, particularly to
the U.S., the Chinese economy is in trouble. Yes, there are risks to confront-
ing China in regard to the renminbi. As time passes it will most likely shine
light on a more difficult problem in confronting China to protect ourselves.
China has excess baggage to carry onto the world stage.

1. It has vast corruptness in its system. For example, it has private pris-
   ons governed by corrupt officials, who steal from those living under
   their jurisdiction.
2. The demographics are devastating. It has become a population of
   males. The government population control program restricts families
   to having only one child. Consequently, they chose a male. The end
   result is obvious; the male will not find a mate. The sociological para-
   doxes are already becoming apparent.
3. When corrected for inflation, the Chinese are not showing much if
   any growth. Extrapolated into a cloudy future, China will most likely
   experience economic setbacks, particularly in the area of the housing
   bubble. However, the Chinese Government is using solid measures
   to prepare for and ameliorate this future perplexing problem. There
   is too much dependence on the U.S. to absorb its output. During the
   Great Recession, much less is domestically consumed. Therefore, as
   the U.S. consumer is more cognizant of their expenditures, exports
   from China decrease. This comes at a time when Chinese labor costs
   are increasing.
4. China is not as mobile as a country should be in attempting to gain
   international stature. Many of the newly created jobs are on or close
   to the shore line. A critical shortage of workers exists in these areas.
   Yet in the vast areas of China, a gigantic and for the most part unemployed, labor force exists.

If compared to China, India has a more slowly growing economy. However, it is more precise. It must gradually shake off the element of socialism,

which is placing a chain on the positive impetus of Capitalism. India only spends 7 percent of its Gross National Product on education. However, as the economy expands, more money, not necessarily a larger percentage will be spent on education. Many in the government recognize this as a necessary for progress. India is in the enviable position of providing excellent education of the amount of expenditures. Here is a country of over one billion people. At the current birth rate, India will surpass the population of China.

In the wake of the economic turmoil in Europe and the corresponding decrease in the value of the Euro, leaves China with trading problems. Europe and the United States are the primary trading partners with China.

In showing our weak side, China is lecturing us on fiscal policies. Yes, a Communist nation is telling us how to run our budget. They are concerned with the projected inflationary problems in the United States and the necessity of having an export market. The Chinese, as the second largest economy, do not want to be robbed by holding U.S. Treasury notes that could rapidly depreciate. It is not unreasonable to assume that the dollar could be devalued by 50%. The strength is dissipated.

Fiat creation of money equals massive inflation. Nowhere is it more threatening that in the US. Lack of economic activity has resulted in deflation. Business must decrease prices in order to sell into a market of decreasing demand. Just look at the housing market. Yet by expanding the money supply, and using massive government credit, and running the printing presses, the political powers, and the Federal Reserve, and the Treasury will, if economic activity increases, create inflation.

How can people who cannot afford many goods and services at deflationary prices participate in an inflationary economic environment?

Consumers are not bidding up the prices of goods and services. Limits on the market places cause producers to cut back both prices and production. Less people working equals less market activity. However, if an expanding government debt increases the money supply, inflation will result.

Some of the limits on economic activity:

1.Lack of credit in the free market place.

Financial institutions are simply not lending and businesses are not borrowing. Going back to Keynes and the marginal efficiency of capitol, business does not borrow when the economic climate is not conducive to generating a profit. The result is fatal to the economy. Capital expenditures, essentially what business pays out for equipment to be used to make a profit, are not being purchased. The negative actions in Government focus on their innate desire to limit economic activity, increase unemployment, and make people more reliant on government. It also has the temporary effect of minimizing inflation.

2. Loss of jobs.

Without money the economy cannot expand. Indeed it is problematic that economic activity will contract. Also the perception that one may have to approach the unemployment line is a sizeable deterrent to splurge at the retail level. Decreases in the consumption function, spreads throughout the economy. The United States is a consumption economy. If people do not have the money to spend, or cannot, or do not use credit to expand the consumption function, the economy will obviously suffer. The ensuing downward spiral will negatively affect everything in its path. Government gimmicks, such as housing credits or car buying credits, will only have a temporary effect. When these expenditures of taxpayer monies are exhausted, the propensity to consume will continue downward.

3.High debt

It is difficult to contribute to an economy when a consumer cannot cope with current bills. Credit card debt is beyond normal comprehension. Foreclosures, residential and commercial, are raging throughout the economy. There is no end in sight. So where is the Troubled Asset Relief Program? The Troubled Asset Relief Program (TARP) money was to also be the problem solver for "foreclosures" - one of the real estate dilemmas. However, the money was earmarked for other seemingly more advantageous endeavors.

Due to unfathomable regulations, banks and other mortgage holders are unable to exercise their discretion in enforcing contracts. The institutions are powerless to act to limit damage. If they cannot collect on current mortgage contracts, why would they lend money to future borrowers? Essentially, the government determines when foreclosures can take place. Efforts to refinance on a wide scale have not helped the aggregate economy. Any type of program has to or will be financed by the taxpayer. To date, none of the government actions have served to alleviate the real estate crisis. It does not have the viability of leveling or containing the price decreases.

Japan, in their crises, in the late 1980s, watched real estate decrease by 87 percent. Japan had a backup. It was their exports to the United States and other countries.

The US is in an economic death spiral. An analysis of the Government's efforts to correct the situation reveals it is on the opposite side of success. Either these people are totally inept or are purposely directing their energies to destroying the well being of the population.

Many of the same people who drummed up the horrible situation are still here to formulate the forces to supposedly generate strength into our economy. How much of a distorted intelligence does one have to have to believe that a good economic outcome can be achieved by the actions of these people? In particular there is Ben Bernanke, (the wizard of the depression economic policies), Lawrence Summers and Timothy Geithner. Alan Greenspan could be tagged as the forerunner of this insanity. Nowhere was there a plan in place to tame down the derivatives market.

Derivatives are crucial in designing a bailout plan to keep the institution solvent. Many bailouts have taken place in 2009. The cost of TARP has been enormous. Yet derivative total in the trillions is more than the total worldwide output of goods and services. Derivatives are a gambling device, which at best are a zero sum game. For example banks can bet on changes in the interest rates - up or down. Guessing wrong may devastate a bank. Some banks even purchases insurance with the view of maintaining solvency. Nevertheless, every time period, depicts an increase in derivatives. The road toward insolvency continues unabated. Failure of these institutions will result in the taxpayer being informed that they are too big to fail. The powers to be allude to global monetary destruction. How believable is this? The benefits, as usual, will accrue to the global central banks, which in turn control the entire economy.

The money supply was over expanded (an understatement). Borrowing reached speculative and fraudulent proportions. With low interest rates, incompetents and persons who could not conceivably repay the loans could borrow with impunity.

Then there was Fannie Mae and Freddie Mac squandering a gigantic amount of money. This was at the time a quasi government organization designed to provide money to loan institutions for the specific purpose of enhancing the availability of funds for real estate purchases. By 2009, Fannie Mae and Freddie Mac became, via takeover, government entities.

Their functions of squandering money did not change. Constantly the taxpayer is obliged to provide funds for these perverted organizations. Bailouts should be thought of as a synonym for dispensing the taxpayer's money to oblivion.

Debauching the currency and attempting to illuminate nonexistent growth, undermines societies standard of living to such a degree, in the present circumstances, that many feel that their capabilities to provide for themselves and their families are in jeopardy. Many are unemployed and are currently unable to maintain any standard of living (obviously). Somehow they feel abandoned to the Stone Age.

Within the global financial system there is close to 600 trillion dollars in derivatives. All of this is waiting to crush the global economy. The bubble is unchecked. Silly regulations (unworkable) are being recommended. The cold fact is that the situation is so far out of hand that the central banks are helpless to intervene in the process.

The etiology of the problem started quite some time ago. Recently it gained momentum to such a degree that it negatively affected vast segments of the population. Many actions caused this debacle, such as collateralized debt obligations or CDOs (sub prime money markets). Considered investments, these obligations were passed from one financial institution to another, without consideration as to the weakness of these mortgages. To assure the return of investment, these institutions insured the collateral debt obligations. Individuals with horrible credit ratings were given mortgages in which they did not have the financial capability of repaying. In addition, interest rates were kept artificially low. As a result builders, benefiting from the government instituted low interest rates, were able to inflate the selling price. Builders were also the beneficiaries of illegal (low priced) labor. So in effect, the indigent Americans were not participants in the work market. All appeared well as the bubble was growing. The bubble fractured, leaving devastation in the financial system. It quickly encompassed to the real estate market and the construction industry. Obviously, as time progressed, it was only the beginning of the economic crises.

A flood of government programs, instead of ameliorating the problems, only made them reach catastrophic proportions.

In the United States, the debt continues to skyrocket to unimaginable proportion. Politicians exclaim that the national debt places a burden on our grandchildren. How can that have any possibilities? It appears not if, but when this once great country will be bankrupt. The attack against our well being is conducted on many fronts. Socialized medical care, and global warming programs, and deficit spending, are just to mention a few.

There are many players in the global and domestic financial destruction. Here is a partial list:

1. Banks
2. Hedge funds
3. Insurance companies
4. Private equity firms
5. Mortgage providers, private and government as in Freddie Mac and Fannie Mae.
6. Government

As the government takes the wrecking ball to our freedom and economic well being, the prospect grows of a run on the financial institution. It happened in September of 2008. Somehow, within a matter of days, the system put itself together. In its wake, it created unimaginable consequence to the highest speculators in the global economy. Nowhere was this more apparent than on the elite institutions on Wall Street, large banks and insurance companies. With rare exceptions, all of the elitist institutions were bailed out by the exclusive use of taxpayer's dollars. The taxpayer was even generous enough to cover those gigantic Christmas bonuses to the top executives. Washington and the elitist Wall Street people and institutions are tied directly in the concerted effort of causing destruction. How do they get away with it?

The stimulus package did not create the million of jobs that were promised. It was a myth, hoax or a lie (take your pick). The stimulus package was never intended to create jobs. On the surface it appears as political payouts, benefiting the bail out firms. As an additional note, where are the promised green jobs? Remember all the statements of promise as to how the stimulus package of close to a trillion dollars was going to solve the unemployment problem? The too big to fail feature in the financial system prompted the TARP program funding.

Proposals are being developed to garner yet another bailout or stimulus package. Dr. Paul Krugman, a noble prize winner for economic endeavors has set forth an explanation as to why we need another stimulus package. Essentially, the initial funding was not sufficient. Therefore, we need to repeat the process. He set forth, as part of the argument, that during the depression of the 1930s, government did not spend enough money. Not withstanding the fact that by 1939 many of President Roosevelt's Cabinet Members succumbed to the inevitable dilemma - much monies had been spent and still jobs have not been created.

Paul Krugman's commentary, published in the Kansas City Star on November 25, 2009, alluded to Obama as being timid in not formulating another one of those New Deal stimulus plans. According to Paul Krugman, the timidity stems from the fear mongers on Wall Street. Within the lock step approach is the demonizing of specific segments of the society.

The last plan has a bankrupting amount of $787 billion dollars. A claim has been made that it saved 6000 jobs. That would be over 1.3 billion per job. Was the 6000 saved jobs the total in the data pool or were there other jobs created? Probably, likely it was a made up figure.

Paul Krugman is the same Economist who during the Bush administration faulted the President for not handing over the TARP money to the Treasury. A few days earlier, the Kingdom did exactly that. Much to their dismay, the banking system failed - many banks went bankrupt taking the Government's stipends with them. The negative effect on the British Pound will be felt in perpetuity. Socialism will reign in the United Kingdom.

Mark Davis, a columnist writing in the Kansas City Star on January 2, 2010, mentioning Paul Krugman in a positive light, as one who criticizes O'Bama and the Congress for passing a stimulus package that was too small.

He continues in his road to riches diatribe:

"Krugman's central message is that government can, should and must fix the economic ills that befall Americans."
"Governments critical role is to keep information flowing, open opportunity broadly, level playing fields and ensure that markets function."

Then as a seemingly oxymoron or contradiction, Mark Davis, alludes to the existence of a clear danger in Washington, making our economic choices.

How many trillions of dollars must be spent by a nation that is already bankrupt? There is not one mention of the negative effects (risk) involved in all of this. History is replete with the catastrophes of following such a policy. During the 1930 depression, Roosevelt in an effort to keep the economy afloat, spent from the U.S. Treasury. It was apparent that the Government, even if well intentioned, cannot conquer the economic ills of a nation. However, it can readily conquer the people and at the same time, expand its perennial objective of moving toward omnipotence.

These people have an out when the objectives fail. Simply, they can state that enough money was not spent by the Government to create economic growth.

Japan, more recently, followed practically the same path. In 1988 it started to transfer debt from individuals to the banking system. It did not write off a gigantically failed debt. Placed in this quandary, the country with the second largest Gross National Product floundered in this self generated abyss of deflation while creating a government debt of such a sizeable magnitude. The individual Japanese now owes more per person, of government debt, than any other indigenous group on the planet. The debt approximates the total output of goods and services for one year (GNP). Its options are limited. Within a short period of time, the economy is decreasing at a faster rate than previous projections. Thus the standard of living for the Japanese will falter. How much further behind can we be?

In a Fox News interview pertaining to possible tax reduction for motivating businesses, Obama said "It is important though, to recognize that if we keep on adding to the debt, even in the midst of this recovery, that at some point people would lose confidence in the U.S. economy in a way that could actually lead to a double-dip recession. This is the same president which spent trillions of dollars in less than a year. The actual national debt is over five times the total output of goods and services (GNP). Yet the President states that people will lose confidence in our economy and Paul Krugman is in favor of spending for another stimulus package.

Why not throw another 2 trillion into the fray and speed up this pathway to bankruptcy?

There is a total lack of understanding, by many, as to the correlation between government taxing and spending, and the subtraction of funds from the free market place. Raising taxes results in a decrease (not increase) of revenues.

The private sector is being demoralized. How can there be any doubt that this administration is, on purpose, driving them out of business by subverting the free enterprises system? Small businesses are the largest employers. Their demise will create a depression. Many small businesses look at the de-motivational elements:

1. Large tax increases from many areas of the Government
2. Unavailability of funds - difficulty in acquiring even short term loans for everyday operations
3. Government demands on businesses even to the extent of providing health care insurance
4. Bleak economic outlook Not much excitement or confidence in another stimulus package
5. Paying out of unemployment insurance
6. Complying with increasing government regulations such as the impending Environmental Protection Agency actions.
7. Government's hostile attitude toward profits.
8. Absence of ability to maintain private property rights

Lingering, ever close is the blowing up of the global financial system. A depression is a possibility. The tragedy of a chain effect wiping out trillions of dollars of wealth lurks as an ever increasing possibility.

Here are some of the potential events:

1. Non functioning, undercapitalized, bank system Businesses cut off from the capitol markets
2. Securities, particularly bonds will be downgraded after the fact. Many will have already have reached the worthless stage as the uninformed or unsuspecting public strives to salvage some dollars.
3. A major market sell off where it feeds on itself on the downside as margin calls are exercised - leverage in reverse. Excess leverage will be sucked out of the market. The derivatives will destroy an uncountable number of institutions.

There is much dangerous thinking out there. Little is questioned or if it is, the matter is relegated to a back stage. At a later time it is finally brought out as a minor item. Government continues with its squander mania. The currency is debauched. Only the lack of effective demand in the market place and the inability of people to acquire loans contain inflation. The inability to have a properly functioning economy, coupled with the lack of desire to "purchase down" the excessive inventories, is deflationary. This is not a contradiction. Take a look at real estate. People are not buying. Therefore, prices are falling. Continually, there is discussion of turning the corner and being on the path to economic recovery. Many obvious false reports of growth are exposed by the news media. Meanwhile those able to envision the reality picture, perhaps envision a Stone Age society. One that is unable to function. The dollar is doomed. The United Nations and other nations known as the gang of 16 want to transplant the dollars as the world's reserve currency. The United States may even pay for this by further funding of the International Monetary Fund.

One of the many goals is to place the public sector in charge. Many of the members of Congress were cajoled or intimidated into passing the 700 billion dollar tarp disaster. It did not pass an initial vote. Next was an enormous amount of money for a stimulus plan that never had a workable strategy. How could this have not been intentional? Trillions of dollars are being used to transition our country into a socialistic or communistic state. Taking over of productive resources from the private sector is moving along at breakneck speed. General Motors and Chrysler are prime examples in the auto industry. In this case the bondholders were taken out of the picture without compensation. In actuality the bonds were confiscated. Chrysler was handed over to Fiat, the Italian manufacturer. What possible business motive could exist for this type of action against the interest of the United States?

It appears as useless to look at these actions, (and many others), as unconstitutional and immoral.

This government, particularly, is an enemy of capitalism. Small business is discouraged from hiring or expanding its operations. Many small businesses are closing. The stimulus plan is without incentives or direction. The people are told of the creation of green jobs and that the trillion dollar stimulus plan is working. The powers to be, point at the retention of State jobs, which if it was not for the plan their specific jobs plan, would have been lost.

The TARP money is now being directed toward another stimulus program. Not bad planning, considering the first plan was a failure. The returned or recovered TARP money was to be, in turn, given back to the Treasury. This was a slush fund, not to be solely used outside of the system for which it was originally intended. Specifically, the appropriations were to be used for averting a banking crisis by keeping the banks solvent to lend money to businesses to continue operations or expand their business and also to purchase toxic loans (really bad loans made by the lenders). The money was never used to buy up the toxic loans. Many of the big banks were forced to take money under Troubled Asset Relief Program. Numerous strings were attached. This was to such a magnitude that the Banks petitioned to pay back the money as soon as possible. The banks did not avail them of the opportunity to lend out the money for economic expansion. In fact many loans were called in or in the alternative not extended. Many businesses depend on their loans for their lifeline. The consequences of being cut off from funds can be fatal.

The dollar different from the yen, is not cash and carries currency. It does not have to be converted by the banks into higher yielding foreign bond holdings. Commercial banks simply borrow from the Treasury at approximately zero percent and receive a return of approximately three percent. Why, in this largess environment, would they lend out money to the public? The certainty of return is paramount. The lack of credit in the economy, not only stigmatizes economic growth, but controls inflation, in the short term- it even contributed to deflation.

The patterns have been ominously set. August 2010, may be a significant month, in that aspirations for an increasing economic outlook, were quelled. Government could no longer invert the statistics and put a positive face on the economic outlook. The multiple factors pointing in the direction on an impending disaster could no longer be hidden. This prompted Ben Bernanke to tally up the monetary tools and proclaim the necessity of saving the economy and preventing deflation at the same time. Herein is a problem of believability.

There is world reliance, for the proper functioning of economies, on the American consumer. The U.S. consumer is out of action. Hobbled by job losses, or the threat of job loss, high debt (credit cards and mortgages), houses falling in value, and a lack of motivation, or better said, bleak outlook on the economy. The bleak outlook transforms to the largest segment employer in the U.S. economy - the small business. Small businesses feel helpless and have developed a dismal outlook predicated upon:

1. Tax increases at both the federal and state level
2. Decrease in consumerism.
3. Extravagance of government programs which are funded by only the printing of money.
4. Health care program. The impact is incalculable. It could be of such dimensions as to put many of the existing small businesses into termination and preclude new businesses from entering the market place.

Clearly, we as voters are unable to drain the sleazy swamp. In a meeting of the worlds leaders in Switzerland in 2003 revealed the bubble bombshell that was forming. When the time came in 2008, the U.S. voter was told that these companies were too big to fail. This was recited by the brain dead executives, some of whom have their hands out for ungodly (gigantic) amounts of money in the form of bonuses.

Saving these companies, with the exception of Lehman Brothers who was destined to be eliminated from the pack, inhibited the ability of new firms to enter the marketplace. Thus, this large segment of competitiveness was eliminated in favor of these firms which gambled our future. They could, because of a reliance on the inept and corrupt segments of the government to bail them out, take sizeable risks.

The Treasury is or should be in a panic. The annual deficit is approaching 1.5 trillion dollars a year. Note here we have the annual deficit, not the total deficit. This is not sustainable. In Washington it is not business as usual. To support the inevitability of inflation, the Federal Government aided by the Federal Reserve, who are not part of the Government, and the Department of Treasury, are printing money as never before in the history of the United States. They have plans to increase the annual 1.5 trillion dollar deficit exponentially. This is, again, obviously the opposite of the dictates of economics. Eventually (and inevitably) the dollar will shrivel under the enormous pressures of inflation. The pressure on prices is, currently, for the most part, dormant. Three factors need to be looked at in this environment of 2010:

1. Inflation is a hidden tax.
2. The government distorts the inflationary figures. They show up, for example, in the price of oil, and commodities including food.
3. The consumer is not buying enough goods and services to place effective demand pressures on prices. The consumer is a major percentage of the economy. One of the drawbacks of the recession is a decrease in consumerism. It feeds on itself as people lose jobs, is forced to payoff debts, and limits their available dollars to necessities. Eventually, a convergence of factors will set forth inflation. It turn, it will make the pain more severe.

The continuing creation of the massive debt will bring this country to its knees. Devaluation and bankruptcy mainly brought about by the Federal Reserve and the Department of the Treasury will create a financial doomsday. Indeed, this is a dangerous economic approach. These economic actions are not an experiment. It appears as being a purposeful act.

Another known Nobel economics laureate, Joseph Stiglitz, noted that the Federal Reserve and the Commercial Banks are lending money at close to zero interest rates without conditions. The availability of funds at these interest rates generates worldwide bubbles. Stiglitz, realizing the high probability of the demise of the dollar, is part of the gang calling for a new world currency. Joseph Stiglitz is for the government ownership of banks.

"Central bankers are a club and they listen to one another. They have their own fads and fashion. So for a while, their fad was monetarism, but it never had the support of economic theory. Then that faded and they went for inflation targeting, then deregulation, which, in the end, caused enormous damage".

Joseph Stiglitz is a Professor on the staff at Columbia University, and chairs a United Nations commission on reforming the global financial system. The UN is inveterately promoting the One World Order or a New World Order.

David Brooks, on the staff of the New York Times, attempts to explain away the main misgivings of Obama by saying that he misread the Nation and its desires for federal "activism". Yet he said Obama is still the most realistic and reasonable major player in Washington. Considering David Brooks and the multiple failures of Obama, it is understandable why he made the statement. It contributes to the process of rhetorical inversion.

He thinks a projective 1.75 trillion deficit is alright. This is illustrative of the attempts on the part of the press to act like Obama is acting prudently. Congress is blatantly violating the Constitution. Obama is not only in compliance with this- he is an outwardly supportive of this transgression.

Indeed, David Brooks is in the minority.

The economy is on the verge of a depression. In fact as of April 2010, the U.S. looks like a gambling casino, wherein, the government is pressing on all sides to eclipse the entire spectrum of our existence.

Again, the same people who made this mess for us are the same people who are pushing us down the metaphorical shaft. Only this time they have Obama alongside.

In approximately 1836, the Rothchilds pointed out that control of nation's finances would give them control over the entire country. The Rothchilds controlled an entire global banking system. Who or what group is in control today? How do they benefit from monetary destruction? Remember the Federal Reserve is not a government agency. The banking system is internationally tied.

Hedge funds earn enormous amounts for their chief executive officers. George Soros, who is perhaps the most influential person in the Obama election, made 4.8 billion dollars for himself in his hedge funds.

The hedge fund is not Soros' only other earnings. No wonder Obama acquired in the vicinity of one billion dollars for his presidential campaign. In exchange, we heard so much about change. Obama gave away approximately two billion dollars of taxpayer money, to Brazil for deep water oil drilling. Here is another action to increase the out of control U.S. debt. George Soros' hedge fund is heavily invested in Brazil. Now is the time, for Obama, to pay back the contributors. George Soros did state that the U.S. banking system should be nationalized. The recent drafting by the Senate (Christopher Dodd, Senate chairman) of a consumer protection bill is actually a radical bill along the lines of the suggestion of George Soros. It expands control of the banks to such a magnitude that they will have to conduct an intricate analysis of impending loans. The banks will be held responsible for any imprudent loans. How can a bank tell if the micromanaging government will determine if a loan falls into the category of "risky"?

Under the guise of consumer protection, the Obama administration is focusing on overtaking the banking system. The major element of socialism is the overtaking of the banks. The reward accruing to the regime is incalculable. As was promised in the administration's presidential campaign, the wealth will be redistributed. Redistributed to whom? Not the poor as one would ordinarily be led to believe, but perhaps, a selected elitist global banking group, who are uniquely organized to use government power to achieve their objectives.

Under the Act, the taxpayer will not be called upon to bail out the too big to fail organizations. No sooner had the act became law, that the too big to fail promise was abandoned. Freddie Mac and Fannie Mae, obviously for the time being were not included with the other entities, were once again bailed out. Freddie Mac and Fannie Mae are constantly bailed out. This is costing the taxpayer billions of dollars each and every month.

Senator Christopher Dodd is a close team player with the Obama administration. Prior to the Obama Presidency, Dodd enabled (actually created it along with Congressman Barney Frank) a vile system which provided real estate funding under the guise of affordable housing. Translated, it provided loans to persons who could not possibly repay them. Thus, the real estate debacle was a primary forerunner of the programs that destroyed the economy.

The Glass-Steagall Act of 1933 separated commercial banking from investment banking and guaranteed bank deposits. It can be said that by definition, commercial banks create money. The abandonment of the Act was complete by 1999. A scant 9 years later, the unregulated system collapsed. It was the cause of global financial destruction. Government had created capitol crises.

Waging war is an expensive affair. The Bush administration's deficits were not really contained. However, the proliferation of spending, into the trillions, did not take place until after the Obama inauguration. Going back a couple of years, when the Democrats came to power in the legislature, the United States started on what appears to be downward spiral. Spending started to accelerate. Deficits started to look as insurmountable. The Fed coupled the crippling spending with extremely low interest rates. Real estate loans were given to persons who could not possibly make the payments. These were packaged off as sub prime loans or derivatives. The exact people who created this fraudulent nonsense, Barney Frank and Christopher Dodd, are now in the process of telling the American people about the merits of the Consumer Protection Act. How do they get away with reigning further damage upon the constituency?

Now we are up to the finance reform bill, which will create more regulations culminating in another Democratic Party power grab. It is also a key element that is put in motion to further destroy the economy. Bankers, because of the threatening nature of the bill, will be predisposed to refrain from making loans. The bill contains many paragraphs which inhibit normal bank functions by making outright threats. It creates a fund of fifty billion dollars.

The current administrations fetish to promote regulation is designed to cripple the economy. The recent history portrays a horrible outlook on the free operation of the market place. This is where the productive side of employment is essential for economic growth. It is being choked off by grotesque regulators.

The finance bill is being sold as consumer protection. It can only cost the consumer. It may provide for a derivative exchange. Another gain for the administrations friends portrayed as Wall Streeters. In the aggregate, derivatives cannot be controlled. They are global in nature and are in excess of an incalculable 600 trillion dollars. As such, it could demolish the entire world finance system over night. Yet Obama is composing articles on why the Consumer Protection Act is needed. It is cleverly set forth as avoiding a depression, holding Wall Street accountable, and putting an end to tax-payer bailouts. Nowhere could any of these talked about goals be achieved by the Consumer Protection Act.

Many statements of corrections or consumer help have been offered by the Obama administration. In this instance, the payday and auto title lend-ers will have to be more forthcoming with their terms and conditions. This is not withstanding the Truth and Lending Act. This consumer problem should have been addressed in prior legislation. Reasonable interest rates should have been established via usury laws.

The politicians seem fit to dissolve our financial resources and develop a false mindset that banks are too big to fail. Money is forthcoming (TARP) to offset the discomfort to the financial institutions - whether they want it or not. Here we have the dictates of the Treasury. One of the many results is a payout of gigantic amounts of money as bonuses. It is easy to end taxpayer bailouts - just don't do it. Yet we are treated like fools. One can only wonder as to how they get away with it. The government shows it is powerless to control these elitists banking institutions. The legislation will not extend to even attempting to gain control over the too big to fail factor. Yet, it will have other banking institutions, outside the elitist groups, contribute 50 bil-lion dollars as insurance against the taxpayer having to bail out the too big to fail banks. Actually this is a proposed tax, which the consumer will have to fund as a result of acquiring a loan.

The wording in the bill leaves too much open-endedness. The terms, such as substantial and significant, are purposely not defined. Thus the rules are not known. The typical CEO, will have to walk through a landmine. The Consumer Protection Act is purposely replete with errors and vague terms; the bill will create many enigmas and corruptness, such a crony system. Institutions, attempting to meet the vague and undefined requirements of the bill will be in a perilous situation, which can only negatively affect the institution's operations.

For example the newly formed bureaucratic commission can request information that lacks limits. These regulators can arbitrarily determine which rules apply or in the alternative develop their own regulations. A

wrong move or guess can result in a giant size fine of two hundred million dollars and a jail sentence. A paragraph in the bill may have a look
back period of five years. An executive who has a good four years of corporate operations, may have a bad fifth year. This could jeopardize five
years of earnings as one may be required to relinquish this amount to the
government under the guise of a penalty. What person could be motivated
to take such an undertaking?

This open-endedness is also deleterious for the consumer. Additional
costs of compliance have to be paid. The ambiguous bill is over one thousand pages. Its benefits are difficult to find. The illusions that it applies to the
large operators are false. They are the elitists who are immune to government regulations. It will provide jobs to many government agencies. The
agency employees in performing their tasks will increase the costs to the
bankers. In their endeavors to comply, the costs will be passed onto the borrowing consumer.

Nowhere is one advocating the premise that regulation is not needed.
It is the magnitude and redundancy of the regulations that serve no meaningful purpose, other than over control of the system. It is in actuality a
prelude to total take over of the banking system. Already we can witness
government take over within this realm, as in student loans. The government can control access to loans and therefore education. There are secretive elements of the bill-for example the Securities Exchange Commission
does not have to reply to citizen's request for information. So much for
transparency and the Freedom of Information act (Public Law 93-579).

The free movement of currency is under attack. New rules will require
foreign banks to report on American citizens. Again, we have regulations
to put teeth into compliance. The currency controls are deviously put into
the hiring bill. It makes no difference that it is unrelated. In fact that is the
objective - to hide it. Foreign banks offsetting this harassment will opt to
not do business with Americans. This in turn will have a negative impact on
exports.

The Euro currency countries are as strong as their weakest link. At the
moment Greece may be the weakest link. If anyone attempts to illustrate
the similarities between Greece and the United States in relation to the run
away budgets, is branded as a person opposed to health care reform (as
they probably are) and wishes to disband programs that take care of the
needy. Social security is thrown into the mix. Paul Krugman, writing an editorial published in the May 16, 2010 edition of the Kansas City Star, probably

believes this is a viable issue. In essence we are better able to cope with our debt.

"True, our debt should have been lower. We'd be better positioned to deal with the current emergency if so much money hadn't been squandered on tax cuts for the rich and an unfunded war. But we still entered the crises in much better shape that the Greeks".

"And we have a clear path to economic recover, while Greece doesn't. The U.S. economy recovers, while Greece doesn't. The U.S. economy has been growing since last summer, thanks to the fiscal stimulus and expansionary policies of the Federal Reserve, finally producing job gains and showing up in revenues. We're on track to match the Congressional Budget Office projections of a substantial rise in tax receipts. Put these tax receipts together with the Obama administration's policies and they imply a sharp fall in the budget deficit over the next few years".

Why are we comparing the Greek economy in the first place? The economies are totally different in operations and size. Where are these jobs that are going to contribute to a fall in the deficit? Look at the projections the Congressional Budget Office made on health care in predicting a surplus. Only later in a clumsily enacted statement, the Congressional Budget Office retracted and realistically concluded that a trillion dollars in additional debt would be added to the U.S. deficit. Now, we are to have a future sharp fall in the deficit. A false emphasis on the nature of the Bush tax cuts was contained in the Paul Krugman editorial.

Paul Krugman continues,

"Bear in mind that the drive to cut taxes largely benefited a small minority of Americans: 39 percent of the benefits of making the Bush Tax cuts permanent would go to the richest 1 percent of the population."

Bear in mind, also, that taxes have lagged behind spending partly thanks to a deliberate political strategy, that of 'starve the beast': Conservatives have deliberately deprived the government of revenue in an attempt to force the spending cuts they now insist are necessary."

Where and when did this deprivation of revenue happen? The economy has not been growing. If anything is growing, it is unemployment, which leads to decreasing tax receipts - both federal and state. The deficits are outrageous and growing at an increasing rate. This is part of the Obama, wreck the economy program. Concomitant with the tax and spend program is the less than an honest assessment of Bush's tax cuts. A sizeable majority of the taxpayers ended up paying zero taxes. More deductions and credits, such as the earned income credit and the child care credits, jettisoned many taxpayers out of paying taxes and becoming recipients. Many of them are illegal aliens who were able to acquire green cards and drivers licenses. Note that as of December 2009 fully 47% do not pay taxes. Again, many of them are recipients receiving tax credits. That leaves 53% of the population paying over 99 % of income taxes. Paul Krugman's tax analysis of the Bush tax cuts appears as being replete of errors.

The International Monetary Fund (IMF) approved forty billion for Greece. This is a down payment for the impending massive bailout of the EURO. Remember, an organization is as strong as its weakest link. The impending disasters of Italy, Portugal, Ireland, and Spain, are not far off on the horizon. Is the World Bank and the International Monetary Fund standing by to raid (with its complicity) the United States Treasury?

Earlier in the Obama administration, Senator Jim DeMint, Republican, North Carolina, objected to IMF funding as requested by the G 20 Finance Ministers and the European Central Bankers The give away program continued unabated as Senator DeMint's amendment to prohibit the IMF from using the U.S. taxpayers. It gets worse, Congress with the prompting of Obama, gave $ 108 billion, to the Central Bank Governors, through a war spending bill. This was not a diversion, but a pass through. Either way it does not matter. Thus, the U.S. taxpayer's money is being used to bolster foreign governments at a time when domestic deficits are increasing at an increasing rate. The Central Bankers along with the Greek government will return to the U.S. Treasury's bank window. It is only a matter of time.

All of this is happening when the memory of the failed $ 700 billion dollar program helped with the foreign bank bailout program. Some of this money will end up in the hands of our enemies, who partially control the IMF disbursements.

Now we have the needy in Greece to bailout via the IMF - a country that embraces corruption. Many of the marchers in the streets of Athens are communists and overpaid government employees, who because of the bail out will be able to have a continuation of the many soft cushioned jobs. This is characterized by, among other things, early lucrative retirement plans, extending to the other indigenous subsidized people, such as artists. Essentially, the population is looking to government to preserve their unaffordable style of living. Because of a practically nonexistent capitalist class of investors who create jobs, the economic pie is limited. The population is constantly looking toward government to perpetuate their existence, instead of taking individual responsibility. To stay in power, the government members dole out these unearned benefits. History shows these grandiose plans, even with lavish funding, do not succeed. The outlook for the EURO is dismal. The system is designed to get worse. Not changing direction has the obvious prescription, to end in disaster. It is only a matter of time.

Columnist and commentator George Will cited critical data relative to the Greek bailout and Americas budget problems.

"America's projected $9.7 trillion in budget deficits in this decade will drive the nation's debt to 90 percent of GDP (Greece's is 124 percent). So some people say that to avoid a Greek style crisis, America should adopt a value- added tax (VAT). But Europe's most troubled nations-the PIIGS: Portugal, Ireland, Italy, Greece and Spain have VAT's of 20 percent, 21 percent and 16 percent, respectively, As part of its austerity penance, the Greek government is going to give itself more money by raising its VAT to 23 percent." (Ref. Kansas City Star, May 15, 2010.)

The profligate spending vastly undermines the economic well being of the U.S. We are aware of all of this. However, we must realize the implications here of having bailed out the EURO and Greece. This encompasses money that we do not have. It ties us more into global currencies which are, with rare exceptions, heading into a catastrophic finale. In the long run, the probability is that Greece will not be saved. It is only a band aid. They are living beyond their means. It is as though they have a right to a high standard of living even though it is not linked to economic production. The bureaucracies are loaded with people who do not produce anything. Simply, government employees do not add to the economy; however, they are naturally adept at subtracting from it by siphoning off capitol which is needed to furnish business with the motivation to generate profits and jobs. It is an essential element to the development of a functioning middle class. A middle class propped up by government employment is doomed to fail. The Greek actions are reminiscent of the continual disaster existing in Argentina.

George Will at an earlier time stated:

"Today there is more Marxists on the Harvard faculty than there are in Eastern Europe."

Republican Congressman, Todd Tiahrt, of Kansas wrote an article in the Kansas City Star, May 19, 2010 edition entitled American Taxpayer Money Shouldn't Go to Greece.

"A short-run bailout will not fix Greece's long-term solutions needed to trim its overstuffed government. Reducing the size and costs of its government addressing regulatory burdens and embracing more free market concepts are practices Greece should immediately adopt to begin recovering from its economic crisis."

This will not happen. People demonstrating in the streets of Athens, some communists and many others are government employees; demand more, not less government actions. In the long term, survival without bailout is not possible. This is the inverse of the Tea Party which demands less government.

Todd Tiahrt in referencing our economic situation continues:

"Congress should have enacted swift and powerful reforms that would have removed barriers to competitiveness and spurred economic growth in all sectors of the economy. Had we used the last two years to engage in meaningful reforms to address regulatory burdens, unsound tax policies, unchecked healthcare costs, rampart lawsuit abuse and onerous energy production restrictions, we could have been on a fast- track recovery timetable with long-term economic benefits. Instead we are in our ninth consecutive month where the national unemployment rate has been at or near 10 percent."

Our bailout programs have extended from domestic to global proportions. Will the Greek Bankers and Bureaucrats get big bonuses and then need a consumer protection plan?

In the United States, the wealth, except for the Washington D.C. area, is dissipating. Here we have a proliferation of contractors, government workers, lawyers and lobbyists. Corporations have to have both lawyers and lobbyists to protect themselves from the ravages of government. In previous times practically all of the energy placed into the system was used to further the self interest of the business. Wealth is being both destroyed and redistributed. The far reaching effects of this debacle should reach its crescendo before too long - perhaps by early 2011. Then our country will take on a totally different look.

Since the inception of the Obama administration, trillions of dollars have exchanged hands. Eighteen months later, the results can be tabulated as being a total failure. For the most part, all of the money is gone. Obama claims that it both created and saved jobs. Continually the Administration talked of green jobs. Millions of jobs have been lost since the inception of the Obama Administration. Taking time to blame the Bush Administration is no longer having a political effect. Apparently, Obama finds this difficult to believe.

Here is a partial list of the statistical data:

1. The Fed purchasing primarily $ 1.7 trillion in terribly bad mortgage bonds.
2. Federal Deposit Insurance Corporation spent $ 300 billion and closed down 100 banks.
3. The Treasury, taking pains to assure the constituency of its projected success, expended $ 300 billion of TARP money, and another $500 billion in programs. In essence, TARP money has been converted into a slush fund, to be used by the Obama Administration. It is beyond the reach of the Legislature. The ability of the Congress to control TART money has been obviated. The Constitution is once again circumvented.
4. Other government agencies have consumed $ 800. billion.
5. Still another $ 3.7 trillion is expensed to the Federal Housing Financial Administration, National Credit Union Administration, Government National Mortgage Association, Federal Housing Administration, Veterans Administration, etc. The $ 3.7 trillion does not include funds contained in the stimulus rescue programs.

The preceding data was compiled and published by Martin Weiss in his Money and Market internet publication in August 2010.

After all of this, we learn of $ 90. billion made available for additional educational funds. The education expenditures under Obama are skyrocketing, along with the costs of other government programs. The additional money spent on education is void of any results.

Just short of 80 percent of the housing industry has been destroyed. Yet, the government continues to push funds into this financial crater, without the slightest chance of success. The future for defaults continues to look worse. Approximately ninety percent of those who refinanced because of an inability to make the initial agreed upon payments have subsequently defaulted on their loans. Many inhabitants are rearranging these lives, without a mortgage, by walking away from their dwellings.

Here is an outline:

1. Loss of jobs without any foreseeable relief
2. Upside down in the mortgages - the debt on the home is much more than the value.
3. Families who could not have possibly lived up to their contractual agreements
4. There are too many homes on the market. The demand function is too weak to take up the slack of the oversupply. Lack of employment opportunities, coupled with the constant increases in foreclosures, is not only a further deterrence for home ownership, but points toward a dismal future in the housing market. Many of those who may want and can afford a home; will put off the decision indefinitely. One reason is the unintended deflationary price structure within the industry. Why but now, when I can buy at a cheaper price in the future?

The complications in the expenditure calculation are impossible to grasp. At best they reflect estimations. It is a purposeful event, designed to serve the Obama Administration.

The exhausted stimulus and TARP funds are cut off from further injections in the economy. Now jobs cannot even be saved. Statistics are not ordinarily exciting. However, these gigantic expenditures have to be an exception.

Pork barrel spending and irresponsible mortgage holdings have further debilitated government's credibility as a positive force. Concentrating on people and the Capitalistic part of the economy as too big to fail, in place of financial institutions, would have had a more positive effect on the outcome. The plans and programs used in this debacle are evident of a desire for failure. The majority of the people, possibly in excess 80 percent, are against these government actions. The results are discernable. In order to move along the unpopular agenda, undemocratic principles and actions need to be formulated. Some of the examples are:

1. Intimidation
2. Lies coupled with inhibiting discussion while singing transparency
3. Subverting rules as in the legislature
4. Using and developing impossible regulations
5. Circumventing laws
6. Promoting non workable programs as successes
7. Rhetorically promoting hope-sacrifice now for this future intangible

If Congress does not act to reinstate the Bush tax cuts, before they expire in December 2010, the U.S. will have another chain around its neck. It will further drag down the domestic economy. However, it may not happen. Anything is possible. The legislature may have it within them to offset the wishes of President Obama.

Interestingly enough, in August of 2010, Timothy Geithner, expressed the continuation of the Bush tax cuts, as it relates to the rich. Timothy Geithner figured the cost at $700 billion over a 10 year period. The fuzzy math does not calculate. According to the Secretary of the Treasury, the money could be spent on "stimulus programs" to aid state and local governments, and support to small businesses. For mathematical thoughts, the application of the taxes applies to those making over $250,000. These are the exact persons who are already paying a gigantic percentage of income taxes.

President Bush, during his terms in office (2000-2008) borrowed more than all of his predecessors combined. Obama jumped into the spending spree by outdoing Bush. With reckless abandonment of any economic principles, Obama drummed up yearly budget deficits that will stretch to over one and a half trillion dollars. Spending cuts are only directed toward defense spending. Concomitant with the objective of weakening the military, spending cuts are only directed toward the military. This would reach deficits of over 10 trillion dollars in ten years. Suppose interest rates increased. Then the payment on the debt would place the deficits even higher. These are only estimates. Mainly because of the vast amount of people out of work who will not be contributing to the government's tax income, the deficit should be significantly higher. These projections assume that the economy will survive all of these shocks. Many countries in the world do not see the dollar as surviving in its current form. If the foreign debt holders, mainly China and Japan, decide to cash in their U.S. debt obligations, the dollar would be immediately destroyed. Think of what will happen in the aftermath.

Instead of finding out what is wrong and make it more efficient, the scenario is to continuing doing the same thing. Here is another definition of insanity. We have crossed over the crossroads. Obama continues down the path of inevitable destruction and still has the audacity to blame Bush.

The Federal Reserve was created in December of 1913. It was one of these stealth deals, gyrating through Congress after many of its members departed for the holidays. President Woodrow Wilson signed the bill. At that point in time, Americans no longer had their own currency.

President Kennedy in 1963 issued real United States Notes without any debt or interest attached. After the death of JFK, the printing of these notes stopped. Now we have to deal with the thought that the global interest Bankers, have enabled themselves to cash in.

Nationalization, of banks, government operation and unopposed control of the productive elements of the country superimposes itself on the aggregate economy. It transgresses socialism, fascism, and communism.

Government is unable to pay its upkeep. To increase its power it believes it must extend control by developing useless programs that seemingly help the desperate and unimaginative elements in our society. Their existence is placed before us, as persons needing help, dragging down the society and placing it under the thumb of the elite select few in government. Capitalism is the enemy. The supporters, some are volunteers, and others are elected members belonging to same party of the regime. All march in lock step, appearing as a thoughtless conglomeration of people.

Keynesian economics is constantly given the spotlight. The controllers cite various elements of Keynesian Economics out of context, showing an unpardonable ignorance and insult to John Maynard Keynes. It portrays government as the one who must save the earth place by deficit spending. Nowhere is it said that government must add to the Treasury during good economic times. Interest rates are determined by a free operating market. These simple relativities are not considered in this policy. Actually the Economist is mentioned only because Keynes fits, in exaggerated terms, their subversive agenda. They lack any intellectual or analytical qualities.

The concept of effective demand is important in understanding and developing a sound economic program. If people do not have the money, they cannot buy the product. Government has come up with the idea that if people get money in their hands, they can and will spend it. A high marginal propensity to consume coupled with capital expenditures are necessary elements for economic growth. Consumerism without capital expenditures has never succeeded. It lacks permanency and fizzles out. The expenditures are wasted. The long run effects are staggering. Entrepreneurs must perceive a profit and react positively in the market place. Instead, currently, the proposed income tax codes will have a detrimental effect on the private sector of the economy. This is just one example of the spite work used to sabotage the economy. That's what is happening. What other explanation could be ruminated? If our government elected members are actually stupid, would they with all of their errors, sometime make a mistake in our favor?

Propaganda evolves into outright pathological lies. It does not matter that you are aware of these inexactitudes. They are in control and have rendered you citizens as helpless. This is the power they have acquired. You are lied to with impunity. The governing, speaking eloquently, subvert the truth. For example, the statement of making the United States energy dependent will happen because of government subsidized expenditures on renewable energy. It cannot fulfill a meaningful segment of our energy needs. What is needed is drilling for oil and digging for coal. Nuclear plants should be immediately constructed. Natural gas is plentiful in this country. Not using our resources serves to weaken our strong United States. This country has a plethora of oil, coal, uranium and natural gas.

Are you ready for another example? The auto industry is in deep trouble. Yet the powers to be want them to build what they call energy efficient automobiles. Ridiculous environmental laws imposed on an ailing industry will only have negative effects. The cost is prohibitive. People will not buy these vehicles. Consequently, the auto industry will be in worse shape. Reliance is made on the lithium battery. Not a good idea when one knows that we must import lithium from a Latin American country that is generally at odds with us. Of course the United States has an excellent source of lithium. Why is this resource not being utilized?

Unions are responsible for a large segment of the destruction of our production. The rust belt, as it is so aptly named, was caused by unionization. Jobs were too expensive to maintain. Workers benefits such as health care, sick pay, remuneration while unemployed, and out of proportion retirement pay, could not keep pace in a competitive world. Corporations were unable to compete. The ordinary union members must have failed to realize this. Job losses began to occur to people who simply wanted health care, a good and consistent job, and a nice retirement income. There is obviously nothing wrong with wanting this slice of the American dream. It's just that it was too excessive in a competitive economy. The unions were perhaps too confrontational with corporate management. Initially it worked well. Union's workers got their raises, the prices of the product were increased and with inflation, the consumer absorbed the price increases. In the automotive and steel industries, competition arrived by way of the Japanese. By the 1980s, it was obvious that the U.S. industries were not going to compete. In fact, in the auto segment, quality declined as prices remained higher than the competition. Eventually, a large segment of the market was lost. Government's favoring of unions was not near enough to keep them viable. Automobiles sold for less than the break even the point. Without alluding to the scales of economy, each unit sold created a loss.

The Japanese, lacking in natural resources, were able to purchase iron ore in the U.S., ship it to their industrial steel manufacturing center Kawasaki, and reship it to the United Sates for a profitable sale. The domestic steel industry did not even modernize. The union workforce decreased by 10% in 2009. There is no end in sight.

General Motors and Chrysler went bankrupt. The bondholders had their investment stolen by the government. Specifically, they were forced to turn in their bonds for worthless stocks as contractual agreements were broken. The U.S. taxpayers' money, amounting to $100 billion was also taken to secure a socialistic policy of acquiring the domestic auto industry. The firm was not liquidated and the proceeds distributed according to the procedures of the bankruptcy courts. Here is a prime example of government depriving investors of their property rights. The bankrupt firms were saved by taxpayer dollars. Inculcated into this mix were bonus stocks given (gratis) to the unions. In hopes of producing and marketing a small car, a substantial equity in Chrysler was handed over to the ever struggling firm of Fiat. How can this help Chrysler? This took a complicated methodology to achieve a failed outcome. Foreign manufacturers now have an open door to dominate the automotive industry. Of note is that GM sales in China are increasing.

Ford did not take any federal government money. They are now successful and apparently have developed future sustainability. Government cannot reverse course. It is incapable of doing right-even if it is not on purpose. At this juncture, not only is this unsustainable, but is made magnifying worse by the controlling legislation, e.g., cap and trade, health care, and finance consumer protection. The consequences of the aggregate legislation are unimaginable. It is a programmed disaster for profits.

Auto regulations are another example of the power grab. The power within these parameters will be to control our mobility. This is yet another advantage to the unwelcome controllers within the government. Moving the Corporate Average Fuel Economy (CAFE) standards regulations up by a few years will have the effect of having to force manufacturers to design, produce and attempt to sell cars Americans do not want. The current changes in regulations require the auto manufacturers to increase fuel efficiency by 30 percent, to 35.5 miles per gallon. Will ethanol, with its inefficiency in producing mileage, be considered in the CAFE standards? Toyota is under the gun for its safety "risks". As such, the giant corporation was fined an inordinate amount of money for not notifying the U.S. government in a timely manner. Toyota had a sizeable recall, yet it is apparent that they did not have a large safety problem. There were not that many cars having safety problems. Apparently, the accelerator stuck causing the vehicle to be uncontrollable. The problem was, except for a few cases, solved by replacing floor mats.

Columnist George Will in an article published in the Kansas City Star on May 15, 2010 wrote an article entitled, "When Government and Corporate America Merge." The editorial pointed out lies told to the public. In this case it was Ed Whitacre, the CEO of General Motors, appearing in a TV advertisement.

"In the commercial, Ed Whitacre says GM has 'repaid our government loan in full.' Rep. Paul Ryan, a Wisconsin Republican, noted that GM used government funds to pay back the government: It 'simply transferred $6.7 billion from one taxpayer-funded TARP account to another'. The government still owns 60.8 percent of GM's common equity, and the Congressional Budget Office projects that the government will lose about $ 34 billion of the $ 82. billion of TARP funds dispersed to the automotive industry."

By August 2010, mysteriously, Ed Whitacre resigned as the chief of GM.

This is not an oversight or misconception. It is outright fraud. Ed Whitacre was selected by Obama to do his bidding. He does not have an automotive background. Consequently, he should be viewed as a bureaucrat. This outlook paints a dim mural for GM and the taxpayer. This can be expected when one considers that dictatorial powers were used to target General Motors and Chrysler for takeover. Bondholders literally had their ownership confiscated from them. The stock became worthless.

It seems as though a minor problem was escalated into a major crisis. The Obama administration has a fetish with crises. It serves as precursor for increasing regulations that created more bureaucracies which enhance government controls. It also (obviously) increases costs to the ones being regulated.

The big guy at Toyota came to apologize, in front of Congress, to the American people. The Japanese are a polite people. The culture requires this characteristic. Yet Congressman, Paul Kanjorski, from Pennsylvania, exclaimed to the Toyota executive that Toyota will pay. Regardless of the magnitude of the situation, this more than implied rudeness bodes negatively for us. It is a slap in the face to the Japanese. One need not have to apply Japanese culture to understand rudeness. Does Congress have an obsession with solving problems by monetary compensation? Look at the repeat of this mannerism when it is applied to the rhetoric of the gulf oil spill.

The economy is heading for an unmitigated disaster. There are many people, based on knowledge and analysis, who are predicting this catastrophic event. The termination of the U.S. economy, as we know it, could reach a termination phase by early next year (2011). Here is why:

1. The deficit is totally out of balance and growing worse. The government actions are designed to keep the budget increasing at an increasing rate. This factor by itself could result in bankruptcy.
2. The Bush tax cuts are set to expire in 2010. Looking at a point in time of June 2010, 47% do not pay any income taxes. This figure excludes the illegal aliens who do not pay any taxes. Another negative dimension is on the welfare side on the personal income tax, such as the earned income credit and the child care credit. Many illegal aliens are benefactors of this provision, which was extended under the Bush tax cuts.
3. The health care bill will absorb a gigantic amount of money out of the economy as taxes. This will happen without a corresponding rendering of medical services. The bill was designed to collect tax money and concern itself with providing medical care at a later time. Why is this

to happen later? One reason pertains to Democratic Representative John Dingle, from Michigan. He states that it takes time to control the people. Another reason may very well be that the medical system will not function sufficiently to provide decent care. Government's goal is to collect taxes, from whatever sources possible, to keep the charade going. The medical care bill is a remote factor in this scheme of things.

4. For all intensive purposes, the cap and trade bill passed early in June 2010. Perhaps it was made easier by the gulf oil disaster. Fifty-four Senators failed to represent us and voted to grant authority of controlling the population to the Environmental Protection Agency. This is under the control of the Executive branch, - not of the legislative branch. Government, being in control of the medical and environmental systems, places itself in the position of being able to dictate every aspect of our lives, while at the same time confiscating our wealth by ridiculous charges and taxes. Now there is a tax on air. There is not any difference between the prescribed charges and taxes. The Constitution is obviated. The benefits do not accrue to the American citizen. Al Gore may become the first Cap and Trade billionaire.

5. Regulation compliance places an enormous burden on business. Even a slight failure to comply could be construed as an act of defiance against the ruling or oversight agencies. Regulators do not perceive one to be innocent. The number of regulations is on an exponential rise. So is the number of regulating agencies. Here the discussion is not about the need for regulation, but generating government jobs and controls that is the unmitigated expansion of government and subsequent control over its citizens.

6. The instigation of more taxes, such as a value added tax, (analogous to a national sales tax), will take even more much needed dollars out of the private sector of the economy. Many government agencies will need to be formed to collect this value added pickpocket scheme.

Any one of the preceding elements would by and in itself be able to cripple the economy to such a magnitude as to dissolve the middle class. We have heard the overuse of words such as unsustainable and a train wreck. In looking at words as symbols, this appears as an excellent choice. In addition to all of this, as pointed out throughout this book, there are many other elements in play.

Paul Krugman and others allude to the Great Depression of the 1930s as a measuring stick of non success of the plans and programs, because the Roosevelt administration did not go far enough in the spending process to offset the economic chaos. Yet it was realized before the end of the 1930s that despite all of the deficient spending, jobs were not created. There are two elements in this process, zero interest rates and massive spending. Japan tried zero interest rates. It did not work for the Japanese and it will not work for us. This is not a matter of probabilities, but of certainty. This started with the collapse of the economy in 1988. By 2000 (or sooner) the average Japanese owed more in government debt than any citizens of other countries. Attempts, in 2010, to increase the sales tax, resulted in a purge of the Democrats in the Japanese Diet. Desperate measures to confront inexorable problems will, in the long term, only add to the disaster. Nowhere is their grasping of the details that can be developed to contribute to solving even a portion of the problem. Politically, any possible positive actions or innovations are promptly dismissed. Sacrifices to reap future benefits are politically unpopular and therefore unworkable. Increasing already high taxes will create a worse situation. Suffering the consequences, which the government cannot control, is an inevitable happening. The longer it takes to work through the system, the worse the effects. For example, part of the spending includes the constant increasing of unemployment benefits. With rare exceptions, the payment is made by employers. Thus, money to be used discretionally to create jobs and other positive activities are absorbed by the government.

There is a penchant to continue to use that which cannot work. History, unequivocally points this out. The United States by the end of 2010 will have a deficit of over 75 percent of its GNP (Gross National Product). No country has ever survived such a financial dilemma. It is mathematically unsustainable.

Repeatable, you hear from people like Paul Krugman to let loose another stimulus package to generate a revival of the economy. The previous $ 787 billion was a fiasco. In actuality, the expenditures have had a decisive opposite effect.

Also repeatedly mentioned are the needy and their need for sustenance. How many trillion dollars have been spent on the needy? Little if anything can be shown to have improved their lot. Nowhere can any efficiency of capital utilization be shown to improve anything. The administration constantly assaults the free market.

George W. Bush is continually mentioned, by the lock steppers, as a cause of the current devastating situation facing America. Yet the 2009 deficit increased to 1.4 trillion, this is 300% more than the Bush deficit. Indeed, Obama is responsible for the terrible situation. The ideology may be found elsewhere, but his programs are driving the population into the ground. The unpopularity with this regime does not have an historical reference. The constant assault on the free market is obviously wrecking the economy and debasing the currency. Many "thinkers" believe the dollar will crash. This would take the economy over the brink and beyond depression. With run away inflation, we would become a fourth world country. The conjuncture is the same as it applies to other so called industrial economies. It is a futile comparison because it does not solve our dilemma. It merely implies that if we are destroyed, so are they. Also, it is futile to look into the philosophies and analysis of the "thinkers. It just doesn't change the perils that are governed by actions.

The anti capitalists blame and slander capitalism by accusing the capitalists of greed and dishonesty. They develop opportunities to promote Socialism and Marxism. The anti capitalists strive toward government control of the means of production. The pricing in the free market place conflicts with the price fixing of the Marxists.

Many of their number accuse people who set forth and question their agenda as conspiracy theorists, or worse, Tea Party people. Yet, one does not have to even engage in careful listening to determine this undermining of the United States. Obama, at the helm of the regime, makes declarative statements which more than suggest his plans (agendas) as President:

1. The redistribution of wealth,
2. Creation of a special internal police force (like it would offset or help the use of the military),
3. Being a nation without borders. Borders and language are two primary factors defining sovereignty.
4. Now is not the time for profits-they will come later. Spoken like a true fascist. Who other than an insane person would invest in an entity that cannot show a profit? Russia used a 5 year plan. It failed so miserably that no one bothered to suggest changing it. Note that innovations, of any sort, never emanated from the U.S.S.R.

CHAPTER 9

THE GULF OF MEXICO FIASCO

At certain times, government has to be relied upon to provide the positive actions necessary to solve crises. The Gulf Oil Spill crisis is a pathetic example of how government operates to solve problems. By any analysis, it is apparent, that government makes matters worse. How could this happen?

The Obama administration and the sycophants, from the beginning, lied about their actions in the Gulf Crisis. Continually, they emphasized having been on the scene from "day one". Yet the President and the administration's personages were nowhere to be found in the region of the Gulf. Acting obliviously appeared as a purposeful act driven by an agenda to create:

1. An expansion of control over British Petroleum, and other petroleum producing corporations, resulting in making negative inroads in the capitalistic systems
2. Closing down drilling for oil
3. More unemployment which will place more reliance on the government
4. An expansion of government via more regulatory agencies
5. A chance to demonize business entity- BP oil

To change the focus of blame from the administration, efforts were directed toward blaming BP and extorting dollars from the corporation. BP is absorbing a multitude of expenses associated with the Gulf debacle including unemployment. Thus, among a plethora of items of expense, the administration was successful at having BP pick up the Gulf crisis unemployment bill.

A travel restriction, which is, flying over the Gulf, has been prohibited by the Obama Administration. A public must not view the economic and ecologically crippling caused inaction the Obama administration. The victims are the inhabitants of the Gulf. It is the matter of seeing failure and incompetence on a grand scale. What happened to transparency? The dictatorial actions of Obama, deprivation of the free press and the disregard of the Appeals Courts decision in the matter of not prohibiting drilling in the gulf, are incomprehensible to those who fail to understand the current reality.

Obama's Gulf Oil Spill emphasized the demonetization of our court system. Regulators are able to transgress court decisions, even the decisions rendered at the Appeals Court level.

A slush fund approximating twenty billion dollars was literally extorted from BP by various threats, such as criminal prosecution. This is one of the primary points in question. It does not obviate the culpability of BP. However, one must consider the government absence of actions to ameliorate the disaster. Instead of helping, the Obama Administration created a multitude of obstacles, which insured a continuing of the devastation. For example, the Coast Guard did not properly respond, but publicly and correctly portrayed BP as the one in charge. When it became apparent that BP was not capable of stopping the oil leak, the government still did not take the initiative. Instead, the Obama sent lawyers to the crisis zone. An analysis of inhibitors characterized by incompetence can only stretch so far. After that, it becomes a purposeful act.

BP is not the only entity singled out for negative criticism, to focus blame away from the administration.

A Republican Representative, Joe Barton, made a sort of apology, to BP for the government's action. Be that as it may, it was not entirely out of line. BP did not do this on purpose. Discourteousness, in this unique disaster, should not have been the modus operandi. This methodology is being used to intimidate BP. It is, again, focusing the blame on BP and away from the government's inaction and inhabitations.

Republican Representative, John Boehner was inserted in the fray by statements claiming that he does not care about the people suffering as a result of BP's oil spill. A change has been made from the Gulf oil spill to BP's oil spill. Why not the Obama oil spill? Here we have a convenience of expression used by the lock steppers. Who in the administration caused the of BP's oil spill to be used in lieu of the Gulf Oil spill?

As a direct result of the Gulf Oil spill, significant facts are coming to light.

1. Deep oil drilling takes place because of government policy prohibiting shallow drilling, such as in Alaska.
2. There is an undeterminable or seemingly inexhaustible amount of oil in the gulf alone.
3. The environmentalists will do anything they can to make the crisis worse than it is, even to the extent of prohibiting actions to ameliorate the incident.

A columnist writing in the Kansas City Star, July 1, 2010, Yael T. Abouhalkah, laconically expressed the message.

"First it was the Republican Joe Barton's ridiculous apology to BP. Now, House Minority Leader John Boehner has made his own stupid comments, this time on the financial regulatory overhaul promoted by President Barack Obama and other Democrats. Said Boehner: 'This is killing an army with a nuclear weapon.' Thanks to Barton and Boehner, the GOP looks as if it doesn't really care that much about the suffering caused by BP's oil spill or about the financial problems caused by Wall Street."

Abouhalkah also takes advantage of his chance to denigrate Wall Street. It is merely another head to chop off. Here we look at undermining any lashing out of the financial regulatory bill. This will incur the wrath of the radical liberal press. Abouhalka is not the only one to formulate stories against Boehner. All have the same previously described theme.

Barbara Shelly, in the continuing distortions, commenting in the July 9, 2010 edition of the Kansas City Star excoriated the Republicans for not extending unemployment benefits. She apparently through deductive reasoning imagined that Republicans viewed the unemployed as villains.

"Of course Congress should extend unemployment benefits. The money will act as a stimulus, stave off foreclosures and keep people from needing other forms of aid".

How far out should the benefits be extended? At the actual projections for economic growth, it could be years into the future. It is easier for these people to provide other peoples money than to adopt principles and actions for job expansion. Nowhere is it mentioned that the money paid out in unemployment comes from the employers. For how long should the benefits be provided? Could it be for life? For a vast amount of employers, both large and small, the cost of unemployment insurance has more than doubled since the Obama administration initiated its "kill jobs" programs. This is a major cost of business that extracts money from the operating structure and is thus a contributing factor in creating unemployment. United States Corporations pay out more in taxes than any other countries - and this costs jobs. In essence the businesses cannot meet the responsibilities of domestic job creation. Many firms find a way around the tax by placing jobs out of the United States. Exported jobs that are not reciprocated into our country are indicative of a diminishing economic system. At least six million jobs have been lost in the private sector since February 2009. The projections, considering the current programs, are for continued decreases in employment.

Obviously, if massive tax increases take place after December 2010, the results will be catastrophic. In addition, note that Congress is circumventing their responsibility and legal obligation to pass a budget. After the November elections, during a so called lame duck session, they plan to pass massive spending programs.

On July 8, 2010, Barbara Shelly, contributed an editorial justifying the recess appointment of Doctor Donald Berwick, by Obama, to take over Medicare and Medicaid Services.

"President Barack Obama on Wednesday named pediatrician, Harvard professor ands health care policy whiz Donald Berwick to run the Centers for Medicare and Medicaid Services. That's the right move. By making the appointment while Congress is in recess, Obama heads off the prolonged grilling Berwick would receive in the nomination hearing and deprives Republican senators such as Pat Roberts of Kansas the chance to make misleading and demagogical statements on health care".

Tolerances for debate and transparency are not existent. The Senate rules should be changed so those individuals seeking nomination from the Senate should not be subjected to questions that could possibly be deemed improper. Is this not reminiscent of the comical Kagan hearings? Note that both are from Harvard. Here is another Harvard link.

Dr. Berwick is for redistribute the wealth and curtailment of medical services. He appears too loath the rich and emphasize that the poor are sicker and therefore need form medical care. Indeed, it is an understatement that this selection needs to be carefully questioned.

Not ironically, at the time of this writing, President Obama came to Kansas City Missouri, to campaign for Robin Carnahan (running for the Senate in Missouri) and visit Smith Electronic Vehicles. Obama exalted the virtues of Smith Electric Vehicles and their "green jobs approach". The firm is held out as a smashing success in the President Obama scheme of things. The firm not only received 32 million dollars from the administration, but in addition, other research and development funds. The up shot is that this firm which he flew into visit just hired their 50th employee. Is this not pathetic? Millions of jobs are lost in the country and yet Obama visits a firm that employees 50 employees at cost of close to one million dollars per employee.

The obvious job killing programs developed by Obama has placed him at odds with the business community. Meddling in the affairs of business, and creating uncertainty in the private sector, has served to view Obama as radically punitive. His expression of hostility toward insurance and oil companies is illustrative of these undesirable tendencies.

Many believe, unknowingly, that capitalism is alright if it is controlled by government. Laws and regulations are promulgated to such a magnitude that severe limitations are imposed upon the private sector. The results depict the characteristics of fascism. Fascism is the other end of the spectrum. Adoption of rules and laws for capitalism to operate in a desirable environment is concomitant with what should be sociological objectives. Government has been crippling Capitalism by inculcating extremes of negative behavior within the aggregate system. Look no further than the housing bubble where government forced financial institutions to made bad loans. The greed in the system carried forward to have these bad loans packaged and sold as good investments. The laws in this instance were obviated. The unfavorable characteristic of greed garnered momentum to cross the line into fraud and illegal manipulations. These transgressions directly led to the bailout programs. In actuality, gifts were prepared and given to the organizations that acted improperly. Thus, we have the bailout program - particularly the too big to fail group. Many of these organizations did, as a result, pay out sizeable bonuses (billions of dollars) to their elite CEO's and accomplices. The American taxpayers paid for the bailout and executive bonuses. The people, who created the mess, are still around making it worse. Now they are audacious enough to pass a bill to further inhibit Capitalism, and call it consumer protection.

We are told that the deepening crises are a result of the European enigma. Look at the internal economy and balance of payments deficit coupled with a severe decrease in productivity.

The Federal Reserve is now (August 2010) purchasing Government debt. The goal is to drive interest rates lower in the area of mortgages and corporate borrowing, or so goes the story. Here is another contrivance that will only culminate in having negative effects. In the space of a month, the government and the fed have had to admit that "things are not improving." In 2009 and early 2010, the Federal Reserve purchased $1.25 trillion in mortgage securities and Treasury bonds. This is a continuation of the failed economic policy. Thus the amount the Government owes to the Federal Reserve is increasing at an increasing rate. The money is created from the printing presses. In other words it is created by the Fed out of the blue and loaned to the government. Much of it is relative to the operation of the Federal Open Market Committee that purchases government securities. The theory is that money will be placed into the hands of commercial banks who will in turn loan out the money. The gloom and doom situation is moving along faster. The Federal Reserve is not a government organization.

The August 2010 bill for $ 26 billion is said to avert 300,000 teachers, police and other security jobs. In actuality it is a payoff to the unions. Nowhere can any rational person believe such nonsense. It is yet another Obama plan under the guise of a bail out. Much of the money will end up in the hands of people making over $ 100,000. a year. It will enhance their teacher's retirement plan. Also we are told by Rep. Jim McDermott, Democrat, and the State of Washington, that the $ 26 billion will not add to the deficit.

"They want to do everything in their power to make certain that President Obama can't get the country going again."

The Republicans do not have to place any obstacles in the path of Obama. By himself he is making certain that the country will not get going again.

Money for this debacle is supposedly going to be raised by taxing multinational corporations and decreasing food stamp payments. What else can citizens are led to believe? Food stamps are now being given to at least 40 million people.

CHAPTER 10

GOVERNMENT MENDACIOUSNESS

ITEM ONE

Iraq didn't have any weapons of mass destruction.

Unless one lives inside of a volcano in Sumatra, they cannot possibly arrive at a conclusion that these weapons did not exist. Iraq was developing nuclear weapons. Apparently the reactors showed up in Syria. The Israelis bombed the Iraq nuclear reactor in oblivion. The press did not report this until a government member in Israel spilled the beans. According to the international press, the reactor came from Korea. It came from France. The Russian reactor was inferior. What ever happened to it? Is anyone even asking? The implements of the weapons of mass destruction were supplied by France, Germany and Russia. Russia is currently supplying the technology to Iran. Our Government is not taking any actions. In fact we have had, a Vice President elect (Joseph Biden), informs Israel on a Pre election visit to learn to live with a nuclear Iran.

ITEM TWO

These aircraft crashes took place during the Clinton administration.

Two aircraft, both 747s, taking off from Kennedy Airport, in New York City ended up in Long Island Sound. One was shot down by a missal; the other was crashed by an Egyptian terrorist, Gamal El-Bartouty. Each cost hundreds of lives.

ITEM THREE

Another aircraft, a government contract to Evergreen Airlines, took off from Cairo West airport bringing our troops home for the holidays, exploded off the runway in Gander Newfoundland in Canada. In all of these crashes, all of the souls on board died.

ITEM FOUR
Shortly after 9/11, another plane was blown out of the sky. This was a flight from Tel Aviv Airport to somewhere in Siberia. It was allegedly hit by a missal somewhere over Russia. The likely event was caused by an explosive device placed on the aircraft at the airport in Tele Aviv. There weren't any survivors.

ITEM FIVE
We reach a new area of deceptions. The stimulus package cannot possibly stimulate. It is not designed to create much employment. The obvious stimulation will be for the supporters of President Obama. How can the powers to be get away with these ostentatious actions?

ITEM SIX
The Department of Homeland Security is an integral part of the New World Order socialists. It is operated as such - totally inefficient. Michael Savage writing in The Savage Nation cited a devastating example as to why a citizen cannot feel secure.

"We ran some drills in October 2000 at the Los Alamos national laboratory in New Mexico. Mock terrorists gained control of sensitive nuclear material, which if detonated, would have endangered significant parts of sever states including New Mexico and Colorado. Whether you are liberal or conservative, gay or straight, black or white, you would have died."

"In an earlier test at the same lab, an army special forces team used a household garden cart to haul away enough weapons-grade uranium to build several nuclear weapons."

Between the events, nothing was done to plug up the security lapses. Why? The public is now aware of many of the security lapses and the insanity associated with reading terrorists their Miranda rights.

Incidentally, Michael Savage was instrumental in pointing out the debacle of the taking over of one of the vital U.S. seaport by Qatar. The new media wrongly stated that it was not the seaport itself, but terminals. Savage should perhaps be credited with the cancellation of the takeover of the port. This was during the Bush administration and may have promulgated the action to preclude Savage from entering England. A visa prohibition usually reserved for terrorists.

<u>**ITEM SEVEN**</u>

Many citizens, in the name of security, at the Airport are met with full body X ray machines. The x rays are intrusive in that they fully expose the body. If this is to be interpreted as a pornographic intrusion on the pre puberty personages, a pedophile framework for prosecution could be formulated. Another government laid that vision or examination of the x ray was limited to specific persons in the airport. However, it was soon revealed that the government was storing these "naked pictures". None other than Janet Napolitano, the Chief of Homeland Security, assured the citizens that the x rays would be destroyed. Then there is the issue of radiation. To further assuage the traveler, Homeland Security, via the manufacturer, set forth that the radiation would be dispersed. One is to conclude that it is a harmless x ray. It this is true, it would be a gigantic medical breakthrough. Imagine undergoing a CAT scan and not having being concerned about radiation exposure.

Remember the campaign contributions totaled in the vicinity of one billion dollars? Many interest groups have to be paid back.

President Obama did inherit a nightmare: however, it cannot be construed to function as a license to taking a wrecking ball to the economy and depriving the constituency of freedoms. The goal is not to save the economy, but to establish population control. There is a positive correlation between increased government expenditures and relinquishments of freedom.

Illegal aliens receive fewer wages. They are unable to compete. Anyway, they consume a giant size number of jobs in the economy and thereby decrease income to the lower class of citizens. Is it any wonder there was a disparity in real income between the classes? The upper class was not subject to displacement by the illegal migrations. The Secretary of Labor is desirous of developing a program to insure that the illegal alien is paid a comparable wage. They will still have the advantage of not paying income taxes.

Now we hear the lies about how the authorities in Washington are fighting the drug traffickers on our boarders and at the same time making sure they remain incompetent in the realm of inhibiting the boarder crossings. The April 2010, Arizona law is demonized, yet it is a follow through of the federal law. Much to the dismay of the State of Arizona, the Federal Government failed to enforce its law. Arizona, faced by lawlessness of drug traffickers, laziness of people who desire to live off the labors of others, mounting unsustainable costs of free medical care and the eventual destruction of the State's economy, placed Arizona in the desperate position of having to initiate the legislation. In comes the Obama administration, along with Attorney General to question its constitutionality and accuse Arizona of fermenting racism by using racial profiling.

Now we have a judge that curtails initiation of major provision of the law on ridiculous legal grounds. It essence, the legal determinations focus upon the courts, that are not only unresponsive to the majority but extend to subverting the justice system. Federalism or the right of states to operate within parameters to serve their constituents is undermined by the constant shifting of power to the central government. The power grab expands the center and diminishes the freedoms and economic well being of its citizens. Prominent persons are traveling abroad to undermine the United States by formulating untrue accusations. The end result has many negative facets. It emboldens our enemies by showing weakness in areas where firm actions are vitally needed. It promotes attempts to perceive our enemies as friends (partners).

After the passing of the Health Care Bill, the Democratic propaganda machine went into high gear. The primary target appears to be, for the time being, the Tea Party people and Sarah Palin. The lock steppers came out in force. Eugene Robinson, a columnist for the Washington Post, wrote that one has the right to protest. He invokes it as a cherished American freedom. Then he exclaims that there is no right to vandalism and the threatening of lives. (No kidding). After this comes Sarah Palin and Tea Party crowd as the culprits who set forth the venom of "paranoid ravings" of right wing nut cases. So there we go into a negative fantasy land, which is obviously orchestrated to offset the successfulness of the Tea Party movement and their diligence in commanding respect by acting responsibly. Despite an orchestrated campaign to paint them as inciting violence by using "incendiary" verbiage and possessing extremist views, the successful Tea Party movement demonstrated their ability to practice diligence. Much to the dismay of the opposing observers, the Tea Party gained in strength (members) and commanded a high degree of respect.

Eugene Robinson titled his article, "TEA PARTY-STYLE RHETORIC BOILS OVER INTO VIOLENCE". (Kansas City Star, 28 March 2010.) Mr. Robinson, in his propaganda style imputed a threat directed at Bart Stupak, by the pro choice people. The threats came on Saturday, and as a result of Congressman Stupak threatening to vote against the Health Care Bill. Then, as was witnessed, Stupak reversed his position. Obama provided cover by later signing an Executive Order restricting spending for abortion. This will be not being operational, as the newly passed legislation takes precedence over an Executive Order. Another mendacious trick dealt out by the White House and in apparent step with the wishes of Stupak. Incidentally, Stupak, previous to all of this fiasco, voted in the affirmative for the funding of abortions. Yet he attempts to present an image of taking a stance against abortion. The Democrats have given a new meaning to the word incendiary.

The British Petroleum oil spill played right into the hands of the Obama administration. Not only did Obama get a chance to demonize BP but to also use the crises to destroy jobs and beef up efforts to promote cap and trade. The administration is void of any energy policy, save to undermine it to such a magnitude as to own or control it. BP executives were placed under criminal as well as civil investigations. The company was forced to suspend dividends and write a check to the government pledging 20 billion dollars toward claims suffered by individuals. Apparently, the methodology adopted for the claims was not moving fast enough. What will happen to the 20 billion dollars? Will it go to the proper persons who suffered economic setbacks as a result of the office spill? How much will go to lawyers to be siphoned off by bureaucrats?

The Obama administration carefully crafted language to circumvent their ineptness in the oil spill. Quite a number of days elapsed before the Obama machine emerged on the Gulf scene and stated to a person that they were there from day one. From day one, became a theme of the regime. Subsequent responses revolved around sending lawyers to the Gulf, Congressional investigations, and interfering with, rather than doing what government is supposed to do in a disastrous situation of this magnitude.

1. Multiple permit requests were not granted. All of which were to set forth actions against the devastations of the spill.
2. BP was left to be the lone wolf in stopping the leak. BP was singled out as the entity to be demonized. They were the butt to be kicked. When their efforts failed, one would think that government, even belatedly, would aggressively attack the oil spill.
3. Assistance was offered by many foreign countries. All were turned down.
4. Needed equipment to preserve the shores and offset the oil devastation was denied or never showed up at the relative locations.

5. The U.S. Navy did not make an appearance. The Coast Guard's activity was restricted. As was stated before, BP was left out there to stop the leak and clean up the mess, while it was demonized. Thus, the citizens of the affected states were further denied help to offset the devastation.

6.The plans and programs, of the administration in placing obstacles into the path of ameliorating the disaster (compounding the disaster), is readily apparent.

7. Imagined and conjured up projections of a catastrophic environmental disaster was used to further the administration goal of diminishing economic activity in the Gulf.

8. Restrictions in fishing

9. Restrictions in drilling in shallow waters or land where oil is readily available and the environmental risks are infinitesimal. This is not only in Alaska, but many other areas in the land mass of the United States or offshore.

10. Prohibiting locals from exercising their initiative in cleaning the shores.

Once the positive news of the oil well being capped appeared, the President seemed unsettled. In Louisiana, the analysis of reality offset felicity. The realization was that the loss of the drilling jobs and employment involving exploration for oil would most likely be permanent. The lifting of the drilling moratorium created a bureaucratic nightmare. The restriction and resulting requirements on the drillers makes it extremely difficult to acquire the necessary permission to proceed. Also many firms have already left the Gulf area to drill elsewhere. The time frame, of the resurgence of the tourist and fishing industries in the Gulf States, is difficult to quantify.

Why are the oil companies drilling miles down, when an abundance of oil is practically on the surface? Efficiency and expediency is being tossed aside. Considering the current technology for discovering and extracting oil, coupled with shale oil and oil tar sands, it becomes apparent that energy importing should be history.

Oil may also be a renewable energy. An objective geological hypothesis needs to be developed and studied. In many instances, wherever drilling is started, there are inexhaustible deposits.

CHAPTER 11

INTERNATIONAL

Continuously the United States is ridiculed and blamed for the world's problems. Ex Presidents like Jimmy Carter call our country stingy. He blames Israel for the ills in the Middle East. Recently Jimmy Carter called whites racist. How come the terrorists escape blame? It becomes indicative of the many administrations, which work energetically against the interest of the United States.

Jimmy Carters main objective is to embarrass America. For a while he did an excellent job. Now he is no longer taken seriously - he embarrasses himself.

With a weak President playing up to our enemies, Israel is more or less on their own. Iran is a nuclear threat to the entire world. What actions will be taken to protect the United States if Iran develops the technology to launch a long range missal capable of reaching the United States or assisting Venezuela in development of a nuclear weapon? Perhaps, the United States is taking the place of Israel as the primary target for nuclear devastation.

Some terrible examples from history demonstrate this very methodology of being on the wrong side or invoking the wrong strategies.

The TET offensive by the North Republic is a randomly selected starting point. The TET offensive led by North's General Giap caused massive casualties on both the citizens and the American military forces. The military was surprised. Intelligence, known in Washington, was apparently withheld from the military. Why? Nevertheless, the military, while suffering excessive casualties, won the battle. In fact the victory was so decisive that North's army was absolutely defeated. The U.S. troops could have walked into North. Our government rejected any resemblance of destroying the enemy. Was one war the powers to be did not want to win.

A short time thereafter General Giap find out he could fight the war in the US press. Much assistance was provided by Walter Cronkite who promulgated the withdrawal, i.e., surrender of US forces. Walter Cronkite, most likely on purpose disregarded the achievement of United States forces in the TET battle. President Lynden Johnson said if he lost Cronkite, he lost the war. This is an incredibly ridiculous statement. If true, the plan for the war was one of surrender. The overriding discussion concerning Vietnam (or any war) is a timely victory. Dragging on a war is a benefit to the enemy. The lack of desire to bring the full force of military power to defeat the enemy is a defeating psychology. The citizens lose their initiative. Radicals forcefully express their views against the war. The military attempts, unsuccessfully, to maintain a high morale. It played out in the aftermath of Vietnam and is once again becoming present. The resemblance relative to Afghanistan is compelling.

In the early sixties, when the initial involvement began, it was evident that this war as well as any war we enter into, needs to be won. Korea was an example of the devastating problems that can emanate from a protracted war, which provides sanctuaries and fails to devastate the enemy. Why should another alternative exist?

During the Reagan Administration, a dire cold war situation existed in Nicaragua. The Communist backed Sandinistas, were pitted against the Contras. The legislative branch cut off the Contra's funding, thus benefiting the Communists. What could have been the motivation to work against the interests of the United States?

HONDURAS

Come to July 2009 and the Honduran situation. President Obama along with his Secretary of State, Hillary Clinton, found themselves on the side of numerous radical dictators, e.g., Hugo Chavez of Venezuela, Fidel Castro of Cuba, and Daniel Ortega of Nicaragua. This is premeditated, not a lack of direction or a demonstration of a lack of knowledge.

The wrong word, coup, was used extravagantly. In actuality, President Zalaya determined, along with Hugo Chavez, that he should be able to change the Constitution by packing the ballot box. Thus, although his term is limited to five years, the President could remain in power. The Supreme Court of Honduras, in accordance with the Constitution and the consent of the Parliament, undertook the task of removing Zalaya from power. These bold actions preserved a constitution and precluded a dictatorial takeover.

The free government of Hondurans has been undermined by an overwhelming number of governments. Including, of course, the United States, who cut off aid, thus negatively affecting the poor people of Honduras? This was only a start. Honduras was attacked by the Obama administration on many fronts. Diplomatic approaches sought to intimidate the Hondurans, and demanded elections in November 2009. This is not withstanding the fact that elections were already meticulously scheduled for November 2009. The Constitution of Honduras is designed to have changes in the Government every five years. The Hondurans determine, via the ballot box, who replaces the current elected members. If this holds up, over the long run, it will be a victory for Democracy and a defeat for Hugo Chavez and the administration of Barack Obama.

The military base at Sato Cano, Honduras, has been directly undermined by the Obama administration. This base covers a multitude of missions, to not only Honduras, but to other countries in Latin America who participate in coordinated military and anti drug activities. Within this realm, Honduras is a country which is friendly to the US and is motivated to participate in ventures that are beneficial to both countries. Sato Cano is our only operational base in all of Latin America. Perhaps one will be constructed in Columbia at a gigantic cost and have multiple restrictions placed by the Columbians. It will probably be outlined in a status of forces agreement. What could the Obama administration have in mind when it teamed up with dictators?

Amnesty International is another left wing organization that follows a somewhat lock step approach. This serves to undermine the "good" that they accomplish. In the case of Honduras, they joined the bandwagon to undermine the freedoms the country was determined to maintain.

Amnesty International recommended to the elected President Porfrio (Pepe) Lobo, the actions he should take to restore law and order in Honduras. Not ironically, law and order continued to exist in Honduras. Pepe was freely elected and sworn into office in January of 2010.

The Miami Herald reporting on 21 January 2010, reported on Lobo having made a deal with the Dominican Republic to accept Zelaya and provide passage from his place of refuge in the Brazilian embassy in the Honduran capitol city of Tegucigalpa.

On the 20 January 2010, it was falsely reported in the Honduran newspaper that Zelaya was offered a position in the Lobo administration. Somewhere it indicates a degree of remaining influence by Zelaya or impulsiveness on the part of the Honduran newspaper media.

To quote in Amnesty International in their targeting of Honduras:

"How devastated the Coup d' Etat has left the country in urgent need of a program of human rights reconstruction, with clear objectives and a time line for completion. If President Lobo wants to restore the rule of law and confidence in his government, he must ensure the abuses of the past seven months are dealt with quickly and effectively".

There was not any "coup". The military was never in charge or attempted to take control over government operations. The Constitutional government of Honduras remained intact. Had the disposed Zalaya remained in power, the government would be under an absolute dictatorship, as the Communist type that exists in Venezuela and Cuba.

Senator Jim Demint of South Carolina in an interview with Rush Limbaugh and published in the November 2009 issue of the Rush Limbaugh Letter depicted the current US administration as a microcosm of what is happening in the world. It appears as an all out effort to destroy Democracy in Honduras. It sells out our allies and appeases our enemies -Russia, Venezuela, Iran, and Nicaragua.

After the successful Honduran elections in November 2009 the State Department of the United States continued through the Ambassador Hugo Lloren to continue its opposition to the freely elected personages in Honduras. The Ambassador, unfortunately, and continued its full support for the constitutionally disposed Mel Zalaya.

Senator Demint also alluded to the necessity of Judeo-Christian values in keeping honesty, integrity, character, responsibility, and the work ethic, within the framework of a constitutionally limited government.

Spain and Colombia, not pretending to be fair weather friends, have terminated diplomatic relations with Honduras. Brazil has worked feverously to undermine Honduras and have Zalaya returned to power.

Venezuela, the primary trouble maker in the Honduran situation, has the highest murder rate in the world. Its people live in constant fear.

Many in Iran desire freedom. At the risk of their lives, they demonstrated against the Government of Iran. The Obama administration could not even assert itself to lend moral support to those people of Iran. Many Iranians are being transformed into oblivion.

Afghanistan has become, not a fight for freedom, but a foot dragging exhibition. The war is inhibiting the Generals from carrying out their strategies to win the war. Lives are being sacrificed at an alarming rate while the White House dithers.

In a recent article appearing in the Stares and Stripes, October 21, 2009 edition, John R. Bolton our former Ambassador to the United Nations, alluded to the significant weakness in our foreign policy and its numerous negative effects.

"Weakness in foreign policy on one region often invites challenges elsewhere, because our adversaries carefully follow diminished American resolve. Similarly, presidential indecisiveness, whether because of internal political struggles, signals that the United States may not respond to international challenges in clear and coherent ways".

The Obama administration moves from one mistake to another. The people are told that it is reshaping our policies. In Afghanistan an impossible list of objectives are presented by President Obama for the General Staff to execute, even though the combat rules of engagement are restrictive and the "troops" needed to carry out the various missions have not been approved by Obama for deployment. Along with this is the problem of the restrictions for gathering intelligence.

Here is a partial list:

1. Protect Afghanistan civilians
2. Train and equip Afghan Army and Police.
3. Reform government
4. Provide economic development
5. Wean Taliban fighters from extremism.

Is this gross ineptness, of a purposeful plan to thwart the United States in its effort to improve our security? How exposed does this policy leave the citizenry of the United States? If the American people look at the reflections of the war as senseless, disenchantment will set in.

John R. Bolton, a former Ambassador to the United Nations, during the George W. Bush administration, noted in an article printed in the Stars and Stripes in October 2009 of the dire perils of not establishing a course of action in Afghanistan.

John R. Bolton goes on to explain the coupling of weakness and indecisiveness proving historically to be a "toxic" combination for the American global endeavors.

Taking particular notice of this weakness are Iran and North Korea. The Obama Administration gave tacit permission for these radicals to do what they want. These lawless nations are above accountability.

Attempted moves to assemble a government group to bargain with the Taliban terrorist group in Afghanistan is not only doomed to failure, but it will perceive a mood of surrender and project the enemy as being more of a military and political force than they are. To attempt to depict the Taliban as a separate entity from Al Qaeda is a dangerously conceived conclusion. Mullah Omar, Taliban leader and religious guide, is the commander of the faithful in the Taliban and Al Qaeda. He is the religious guide.

The government of Afghanistan, headed by Karzai, has completed a summersault in his endeavor to maintain his corrupt government and extricate dollars from the United States. On numerous occasions Karzai has attempted to garner the support of the Taliban by compromising in some sort of a peace accord. Not exactly rapprochement, but definitely against the interest of the U.S. The corrupt election of Karzai vastly diminishes our, and NATO's ability to gain the confidence and subsequent assistance of the Afghanistan people. NATO and the U.S. cannot continue to demonstrate complicity with the Karzai government and act like the outcome in Afghanistan depends on this culprit. Success in Afghanistan depends on initiatives centered on military measures, and independence of the current Afghanistan regime. The emphasis should be on military success. This is something the Afghanistan people could depend on. The current strategies are not achievable.

Here are some of the factors which can inhibit the much sought after cooperation:

1. The limited objectives and time factors of military operation. If the U.S. departs Afghanistan prematurely, a vacuum will be immediately created. One consequence will be to leave anyone who even appeared

to cooperate with foreign forces in a life peril situation. Internet sites have become an enigma, in that somehow certain individuals have acquired classified and secret information. There was no hesitation in publishing the information on the internet. The printed versions from the internet of secret documents is a set back to vital military objectives. For one thing, revelations of Afghanis cooperating with NATO, invites retaliation by the Taliban.

2. The indigenous people must envision a victorious U.S. They cannot look forward to a future that places them at the mercy of terrorist organizations like the Taliban or a corrupt Afghanistan government. Currently, it is a detriment to selling the idea of Democracy. Fear of government is the antithesis of Democracy. A corrupt government cannot exist without fear. Indeed, there is a difficult path ahead-one that will require motivational planning and long term commitment. Americans do not like to commit to long term. They desire instant results. The plan in meeting its objective must include decisive immediate achievements-one in which two things happen. Karzai appears to be on a crash plan to formulate a deal with the Taliban.

3. Limited NATO casualties in clashes with terrorists-meaning fast changes in the rules of engagement to include use of technological systems and more air involvement. The military leaders, not politicians, should be in charge-not like in Vietnam. In August 2010, General Petraeus, issued a directive asserting troops rights to defend them, but they must refrain from calling for air strikes or artillery unless it is certain that no civilians are present. How can one be certain of this? How can the Taliban be distinguished from civilians? The Taliban are, of course, aware of this and are able to engage US warriors from civilian areas. Also, the enemy uses civilians as human shields. A good tactic learned from Hamas in Gaza. Civilian casualties are a fact of life for the enemy. Winning hearts and minds is not one of their objectives. The enemy is not saddled with this burden. It is the inverse - our Generals are burdened by this unworkable policy. Again we have an example of Generals who are prohibited from waging war. Winning the hearts and minds of people is not a winning military strategy. Some will remark that diplomacy is the answer. Further, a military solution is not possible. Well, a diplomatic solution is not possible. Translated, any attempts at successful negotiations will have to take place from a position of strength. Allowing Karzai to contemplate

approaching the Taliban signals a big positive for them. It is viewed as Karzai preparing for the departure of NATO from Afghanistan and developing a favorable outcome for him.

4. Is there an end in sight, wherein achievement of goals can equal extraction of military forces? Here is where the Afghanistan people, despite obstacles, can create an environment to undertake responsibilities necessary to operate a sovereign state. The difficulty is enhanced by not developing proper initiatives. Building schools while undertaking additional military risks by altering the combat rules of engagement demonstrates a total lack of understanding of war by the Obama administration. Likewise attempting to burn the poppy seed fields and have vegetables planted is not a winning scenario. The resources needed to even attempt success in the drug area are enormous. Many Afghans make their living from selling the poppy seed. Why would they want to change their scope of business? It appears as a noble goal, but not one that exudes cooperation among the Afghans. Concentration needs to conform to the objective of defeating the terrorists.

5. Pakistan views the U.S. as being weak and not in control of the war. Therefore, they are taking the path of least resistance, at least in their view. Actually, it is presented to them in this fashion by the United States. Pakistan's fight is with India, not other entities. The Taliban have a gifted sanctuary in Pakistan, and are therefore able to cross the border into Afghanistan at will. The sanctuary (surrogate attack force into Afghanistan) coupled with the U.S. overwhelming restrictions (rules of engagement), and the announcement to depart the war zone within a short time span, spell disaster for the United States forces. No one, whether from Pakistan or Afghanistan, wants to be on the losing side. It could cost them their lives. If the opposite was a truism, the probabilities would appear to favor the populations siding with the United States. However, in view of the pacifist and appeasement policies of President Obama, the opposite is true.

Pakistan has taken a further step in its foreign policy approach toward the United States, in closing its border to Afghanistan. Pakistan temporarily terminated the supply line through Pakistan to Afghanistan. It is an exercise in the audacious undertaking of interfering with vital logistics. Pakistan is such a weak state that it fears for its own security. A non response by the United States and NATO, declares to our enemies, that we will not take the critical defense measures to protect ourselves or our allies. New low ebb in our history has been established in Afghanistan by the Obama Administration. Even the opening of the border cannot undo the damage done. It questions the allegiance of Pakistan. In looking at the conduct in the prosecution of the war, the outcome will no doubt be tragic. This means added casualties, i.e., casualties that could have been avoided.

The preceding is obviously not ideal. One may then set forth a formidable alternative. The current approach, for an innumerable number of reasons, appears as doomed to fail. From a strategy standpoint it looks to be on purpose. General Mc Crystal may have had second thoughts on the non strategy situation in Afghanistan. Perhaps he involved himself and his staff in discussions about the ineptness of the administration on purposes (the Rolling Stone article, July 2010). To the casual observer, it may have developed into a method of disassociation from the political handling of the war. General Mc Crystal background is that of a military leader and warrior. Perhaps he felt that future reflections on his career, as a result of a politically controlled war, would be negative. Also, there is the possibility of future psychological pressures by committing personal into combat situations under the politically established rules of engagement.

Upon introspection into the Obama Administration, three points need to be mentioned.

1. The administration appears to be seriously involved in undermining the military as a strong fighting unit. This would involve tackling those individual leaders who demonstrate an indefatigable effort directed toward decisive military victory. After all, this is the viable goal of the military.
2. The comparison by the administration and member of the press into the firing of General Mc Arthur by Harry S. Truman. Not even a reasonable comparison exists. The General was insubordinate to the President on numerous occasions. He steadfastly wanted to attack the Chinese and never backed off from his stance. On occasion he was rude to the President. It was the constant "push", in extending the war, coupled with insubordination that led to his firing. Contrary to the press releases at the time, there was not any political fallout from this decision. General Mc Arthur addressed Congress and had a ticker

tape parade as a war hero in New York. President Truman's decision in late 1950 was regarded as correct. Given this scenario, how can this be related to the Mc Crystal firing?

3. The selection of General Petraeus to replace Mc Crystal was said to be "brilliant". It was repeated over and over to the extent of nauseating redundancy. This was the same General, who earlier in his career, testifying before Congress, was treated with distain by many of the same Democrats who called Obama's selection as brilliant.

Japan is an example of a country that needs to be concerned. North Korea is launching its missiles over Japan's territory and threatening its sovereignty.

Does Obama believe that conversion is possible or a buyout agreement (bribe) can be achieved?

Russia is expanding their military. This nation, for example, is building intercontinental missiles. At the same time, President Obama, promised the Russian President Medvedev that he would reduce nuclear weapons. He further destroyed relations with our friends, Poland and the Czech Republic. Specifically he terminated the missile defense systems in their countries. Unilateralism is a treacherous policy. The weakness is too apparent. He apologizes for the actions of the United States. It provides motivational energies for Dimity Medvedev and Vladimir Putin to reach out to enslave the sovereign states that during the cold war comprised Soviet hegemony under the banner of the USSR.

Medvedev has an open ticket to expand the Russian Empire and gain total hegemony over its former territories. Secretary of State, Hilary Clinton, early in the administration, sought to reset Russian relations. The insinuation was that this needed to be done because somewhere along the line we had not lived up to expectations-a reflection that the Bush administration was at fault and destroyed cooperation.

Resetting policy toward Russia is within itself, deleterious. It was bad enough at the start of this administration. Look at the aggressiveness of Russia in invading the sovereign nation of Georgia. A country on the favorable side of the free world is overpowered and neutralized by a Russian nation determined to expand its influence by force. The reset plan further invigorates the aggressor. Without firm actions, the concessions given Russia are doomed to backfire. Thus, Russia can expand their nuclear capability and use whatever they have at their disposal, (energy in the form of natural, gas and oil), to intimidate their neighbors. They know the Obama Administration will not oppose them.

The U.S. technology advantage is dissipated. Beyond this is a concerted effort to undermine our technological efforts. The goal appears to have our adversaries as technological equals.

ISRAEL

Isi Leibler writing a column in the Jerusalem Post on March 16th 2010 addressed the problem of relations between the United States, Israel and the Middle Eastern Nations.

"Yet this strategy of 'engaging' Islamic rogue states has been disastrous. The effort to prevent nuclear development in Iran by appeasing the Iranian tyrants backfired with the ayatollahs literally mocking the U.S. The response of Syrian President Bashar Assad to U.S. groveling and the appointment of an ambassador to Damascus, was to host a summit with Iranian President Mahmoud Ahmadinejad and Hizbullah terrorist leader Hassan Nasrallah and ridicule the U.S. demand that he curtail his relationship with Iran. President Obama did not consider this 'insulting' prompting the editor of the Lebanese the Daily Star to say that 'the Obama administration these days provokes little confidence in its allies and even less fear in its adversaries".

This is written at a time when Israel is unwavering in its construction of dwellings in East Jerusalem. For the United States it creates an inexorable problem. It exposes the U.S. approach in the Middle East as being weak. It is helpless in attempting to have Israel stop the East Jerusalem construction plan.

Obama developed a schizoid reaction toward Netanyahu. Welcoming him on a visit to Washington D.D. came after both avoiding and insulting him on a previous visit. The act is reminiscent of street type behavior.

The U.S. is perceived as weak. The foreign policy is grasping at straws to stay alive. In the aftermath of the construction in Jerusalem, Hillary Clinton visited Moscow in a vain effort to persuade the Russians to join the United States, and perhaps certain countries in the European Union, against the Iranian nuclear weapons threat. A couple of weeks before this visiting episode, Clinton stated that Russia would support such an initiative in the United Nations Security Council. It was approximately one half hour before the statement that Russian television (RT) announced that it would not support such a move for sanctions in the UN Security Council. In fact Russia never considered doing such a thing.

Netanyahu was on a visit to Moscow to solicit the help of the Russians, in curbing Iran's pursuit of nuclear weapons. He was unequivocally informed of the situation. This indecently, is a long lasting position of the Medvedev government.

Concomitant with the Obama administration is supposedly an objective to rid the world of nuclear weapons. Yet it is toothless in developing an attempt to limit the proliferation of nuclear weapons in the extreme radical nations of North Korea and Iran. Apparently, Secretary of State Hillary Clinton alluded to her having reached some sort of a nuclear agreement with the Russians. Every time this has happened in the recent past, it has been to our detriment. Last time the Obama administration, as a concession to the Russians, abandoned its nuclear defense system plans in Eastern Europe. Thus, a giant sized bargaining chip has unilaterally been removed from the metaphorical table.

Nothing was received by the U.S. in return for actions designed to ameliorate the nuclear situation with Russia. The nuclear agreement with Russia is not an update of the START treaty. There is nothing in this but a relapse in U.S. nuclear strength. Many of the so called compromises are one sided and obviously inhibiting our security. A system to determine Russian compliance does not exist. What is the idea or goal behind these actions?

Venezuela, backed by a two billion dollar equivalent loan, from Russia, is pursuing nuclear weapons. The money for this proliferation will be used to purchase equipment and technology from Russia. Perhaps we no longer have to concern ourselves with a North Korean or Iranian nuclear attack. The ultimate attack could come from Venezuela.

A big group of world leaders descended on Washington for a meeting to address the nuclear issues. So far there are not any "good" inputs to solve this inexorable problem. Again, as with so many other meetings, like the Copenhagen global warming gathering, terminated with glowing statements and a lack of accomplishments.

Cynthia Tucker, unable to resist, a nuclear statement, presented her opinion in the Atlanta Constitution, titled; "The End of Nukes is nearer." The theme is predicated upon the Obama leadership directed efforts toward the security of a world without nuclear weapons. Who would not in the freedom loving world desire this outcome? Why are these lock steppers all in accord with the acquiescence of the United States? The wording in these editorials is essentially identical. They cannot be this naive to believe if we abandon our security initiatives; the enemies of the United States will do the same.

To further quote Cynthia Tucker:

"The United States can never hope to persuade other countries to forego development of nuclear weapons if we remain committed to a bristling arsenal, refreshed every 20 years or so by new technology". "Obama's interest in reducing the world's nuclear capacity also helps to reinvigorate an effort that hasn't gotten the attention it deserves: keeping nukes out of the hands of terrorists". "Despite the modest changes Obama has made in U.S. nuclear policy, he's already facing a barrage of criticism from conservatives, who, predictably argue the president's proposals will embolden our enemies and make us weaker. In fact Obama's policy revision and treaty proposals are less dramatic than I would have liked, since they take only small steps away from our Cold War posture".

So here we have an inverted situation, which is typical of the far left. The Iranian terrorist state is on a roll in developing their nuclear weapons. Note that this is in concert with Russian assistance. This is same Russian consortium that has agreed to a nuclear treaty with the United States. Russia has a track record of not living up to their international agreements. Even if this is a realistic treaty, it cannot be monitored. The criticism is not confined to conservatives. It spreads into many facets of our society. People are not fooled into the belief that this methodology could possible work. Further, a majority of the population believe that we are placed in a situation that is more dangerous. Yes, our enemies are already emboldened and probably further motivated to destroy us.

For years we had the mutually assured destruction (MAD) understanding, wherein, an attack on the United States would result in retaliation. This kept peace in many areas of the globe over the last sixty years. Now this vital element to our security has been unilaterally abandoned. What could possibly be the motivation behind this surrendering of the United States as a world power?

Iran has unequivocally stated that it will annihilate Israel. These radicals are coming to believe that if they launch a nuclear attack against Israel, that they will not face retaliation. So much for a nuclear treaty believed to promote a nuclear free world. Proliferation moves ahead unabated. Obama has set forth a policy that practically assures Iran of a non response from the free world.

Obama had even released or lifted the classification of millions of documents. This handing out of secrets will have a vast negative effect on our security. It will be difficult to recruit help. It is undeterminable how many people paid the supreme price. This cannot be tucked away as incompetence or a ghastly mistake.

Turkey is pursuing a policy that is flaunting its disrespect for the U.S. Unmoved in its pursuit of this objective; Turkey's leaders not only support the Flotilla episodes, but have played up the lies directed at both the United States and Israel. Both are accused of committing grotesque atrocities in Iraq.

E. Thomas McClanahan writing a commentary in the Kansas City Star, June 13,2010 entitled, OBAMA IGNORED CLEAR SIGNALS FROM ERDOGAN, (Turkey's President).

"Turkey, it seems, has been slipping out of the Western orbit for some time, but up to now this shift has taken place largely below the headlines. Its connivance in the flotilla charade-which was less about delivering aid than in provoking a confrontation with Israel-was a loud proclamation of its transformed worldview".

The weakening policy of President Obama is gyrating into an international nightmare. At no time in our recent history can we determine a greater need for leadership. Instead we have a docile appeaser who opposes every interest of the United States. He even apologizes for our action, much of which enhances freedom. The appeasement process is such a motivator that it will generate aggressive military action against the United States and our allies. Obama has deserted Israel. Not only has this nation been discarded as one of our allies, it may now be viewed, by Obama, as an enemy. Nevertheless, they are exposed as having to be solely responsible for their own defense (survival).

The results of the peace meeting of September 2010 between Israel and Palestine are now exposed as a hoax. That is, there was not the slightest chance of success. It was a bazaar opportunity to depict Israel as the culprit because it they did not cease construction of family units in the West bank.

Obama acting as a supplicant is overseeing a downward spiral in the U.S. world influence.

Iran is moving at its fastest possible speed to complete its nuclear weapons programs, and make itself a viable nuclear threat. Coupled with this is its threat to accompany the next Flotilla bound for Israel. Turkey has surrounded itself as a supporter and ally of Iran. Brazil has turned totally against the U.S. Venezuela and Brazil are become ardent supporters of Iran. All this takes place at a time when Karzai is conducting secret negotiations with the Taliban. It cannot be too secret if we know about it.

Think of Mexico and open borders comes to mind. The federal government is not enforcing control of the borders. In fact it is promoting open borders. Washington will fight anyone who attempts to enforce the federal laws. Arizona is the case in point. The judicial system demonstrated its powers against the American people by having District Court Judge Bolton subvert the Constitution in opposition to the Arizona statute and thereby depriving the people of Arizona their right to protect themselves. This is but one element of deprivation. The citizens of Arizona (and elsewhere) are being stopped from fighting the adversary (particularly drug dealers).

There are many who need to be confronted for their opposition to enforcement of the laws of the United States. As an example of persons here in this country that is deleterious to our ideals are organizations. As an example, La Raza, and LULAC, very well organized in California, is calling for a boycott of Arizona. Members of these organizations have openly called for a Revolution in the United States. One of their speakers proclaimed Hugo Chavez and other dictators in Latin American as being on their side in this Revolution. It is more alarming that the speaker was a Los Angeles school teacher. The infiltration is large and insidious.

Mexico is in a civil war it cannot afford to lose. Yet in its current condition, it lacks the resources to win. The drug cartels are taking over the country. The expansion employs such methodologies as imposition of fees (taxes), and extortion with the goal of domination. The end result could be a country run by violent criminals known as drug lord cartels. The spill over effect into the United States is already alarming. The cartels have viewed the open borders as a lucrative expansion of their goals.

HAITI

Haiti received, as a result of a devastating earthquake, many millions of dollars. Despite all of these donations, Haiti remains a poverty stricken country. Corrupt and ineffectual government does not provide even a modicum of services. The country is doomed to poverty. Efforts of non government employees, aid groups and the United Nations have not made a dent in stemming the trend. In fact the United Nations has made a significant income from grabbing money allocated to Haiti. Looking from another prospective, without being able to participate in free market environment, like attracting investment, acquiring loans and developing businesses, Haiti is doomed to failure. Even in the United States, funds designated for Haiti have never reached this country.

The preceding dilemma can be attributed to other countries that foster crippling environments. Dictators steal any resemblance of wealth. The list is vast and endless.

The Jerusalem Post (November 3, 2010), aptly covered the news of Obama opening up the United States to the United Nations Human Rights Council (UNHRC).

The United States is submitting its human rights record to the scrutiny of other nations. This includes, of course, allies and adversaries. For the first time, the Obama Administration plants itself at the foot of a committee, determined to undermine and embarrass the United States, in the eyes of the world. It will open the question of torture in the war on terror. No doubt it will include, among other things, the supposed failure to close the prison at Guantanamo Bay. The other subjects to be brought before the UNHRC will be the treatment of racial minorities in the U.S. and religious freedoms. You can bet on it.

Human rights organizations say the ultimate test will be in the response to recommendations from any of the United Nations, 192 members, including diabolical nations such as Iran.

James Dakwar, the ACLU director of Human Rights programs. He states that the U.S. matches rhetoric with concrete domestic policies and action.

Eileen Chanberlain Donahue, U.S. Ambassador to the Human Rights Council states that the U.S. needs to be willing to hear critisism also from its critics in order to be a good role model. Further statements were made to the effect of our willingness to improve as a result or serious and real input from the member nations.

Improve what? We are at war and exercising unreasonable restraint, which is costing us military casualties. Here is another invsersion, where this administration is pressing hard to undermine (subvert) our country. It does not take much thought to see through all of this. When it is that the crossing of the line becomes sedition? What torture is taking place at Guantanamo or any other place in the world by the United States? The accurization has been set forth by the ACLU, and other radical organizations and individuals, determined to promote their agenda of "taking down" the United States. Interrogations and water boarding had been set forth by these people as crossing the line of civility and thus being classified as torture.

Considering the Obama agenda, this was an excellent opportunity to undermine America. The UN fiasco comes at a time when the News concentration is on the post election. The main news media can interview Nancy Pelosi and thus eliminate much of the information it does not wish to report. All of this is in unison with the lock step approach.

Civil rights and human rights are terms used to control an unsuspecting American population. These terrible weapons are predominately domestic. However, since the onset of the Obama Administration, they have taken on Global significance.

It is not a paradox that China inhibits investigations into human rights abuses. This extends in other states, like Myanmar. China pulled out all stops to preclude the United Nations from investigating the human rights abuses (torture) in Myanmar.

CHAPTER 12

MILITARY AND FOREIGN POLICY

There is a concerted effort to undermine the military and relegate it to an organization that is no better than mediocre.

The military budget is being cut into shreds. Security is seriously jeopardized and getting worse.

1. The killing of the funding for the much needed F22 fighter. The current fighters are 24 years old and need replacing. Obama talks about a future aircraft - the F35 to fulfill the U.S. defense requirement. A move designed to lead the public astray. The administration would not develop the plans, and programs to provide the necessary inventory required to make this a viable part of the U.S. military. Russia is turning out the Talon, which is essentially comparable to the F22. From where did Russia acquire the technology? Consider that Russia will have a superior fighter jet than the U.S. Here is another step in the inveterate efforts comprising the weakening process. The F35 is being packaged and sold to Israel. The secret technology of the fighter must be safeguarded. Does Israel have this capability? What is the probability of Russia acquiring the F35 technology?

2. The termination of the defense contract on nuclear missal interceptors comes at a time when North Korea is advancing their nuclear destruction efforts. Hawaii may likely be a selected target. What if North Korea perceives the U.S. as weak enough not to retaliate?

3. NASA is being restricted in the ever evolving human space activity. The funding has disappeared. The funding for the Satellite shuttle has dried up. Russia is being paid a kings ransom by the U.S. to

place our astronauts on the man orbiting lab. This comes at a time when Obama is talking about going to an asteroid and Mars. Here in another inverted statement. Where is the plan for such an endeavor?

It is not ironic that their programs are technological progressions that have vast future implications for our country. It is a major element in the tightening of the metaphorical noose.

Innovations are undermined by the negative actions of government programs. Eighty percent of the Gross National Product is composed of production. This figure is declining. Decreasing production translates into a decline in the standard of living.

President Obama receives a Nobel Peace Prize. Many events depict this as perverse. Lack of strength (resolve) promotes aggression (terrorism).

It excites the enemy into action.

The "prize" was given to a person who is the world's biggest proponent of abortion. One can only guess that showing international weakness would promote peace among the terrorists who hate us.

Diplomatic initiatives are viewed by the enemy as a weakness. We live in a world where the United States is being continually tested and probed for weaknesses.

The attempt to move toward a nuclear free environment is an antithesis. Showing weakness in the face of the belligerent nations actually promotes nuclear proliferation. This weapon of war is accelerating at an unprecedented pace.

North Korea, in its quest to promote nuclear terrorism, moves forward, unabated. The administration barely acknowledges the missiles flying over Japan. The prestige of the United States as a protector of the free World (Japan for example) is waning at an increasing rate.

Socialists (communists?) in the United States do not have any use for the military. For one thing, these socialists want the Pentagon's money for their hand out programs. For another, their antics are diametrically opposed to that of the citizens. Could this prompt the military to be perceived as a threat? One of the elements that subtracts from the greatness of the United States is to have control of the military in the hands of these un-American people. Yet the concept of the election system cannot be obviated. The military, in our system of government, has to remain under civilian control. A proposal to the contrary is not a plausible alternative.

Viable weapons systems are cut from the budget, without regard as to how they fit into the defense of the United States. The military industrial complex is an expensive operation. It spends many dollars. Some of this is wasted, thus subtracting from the potential military effectiveness of the United States. Administration coupled with accountability for fund expenditures appears as purposely insufficient.

The current foreign policy of meeting with the enemy is undermining our strength. First it gives credence to these sociological misfits as having elements of credibility. It is viewed by the adversary as weakness. It emboldens them.

Iran is fighting for time to develop nuclear weapons. Imagine the glee to be able to garner more time without the possibility of real confrontation. Even Russia is pitching in, with nuclear support and their latest S300 missiles.

North Korea is another radical State making rapid progress on its nuclear program. The United States looks weak on this gigantic threat to our existence. Our allies, like Japan, are or should be in a panic. They were slow to realize that they can no longer depend on the U.S. For example, the Obama lack of reaction to North Koreas launching missiles over Japan depicts a decisive weakness, which undermines the strength and tenacity of the U.S. to act decisively.

The torpedoing of a South Korean ship by a North Korean submarine places the South Koreans on a war footing. This volatile situation shows the weakened response by the United States. The warning rhetoric of Hillary Clinton is subjugated to inaction as it portrays the U.S. in a passive role, while South Korea, being abandoned, is aware of their going it alone role. China chimes in with useless words. As we are aware, China is on the side of North Korea. Nothing has changed from 1950. Earlier in the administration's existence, China challenged American warships off the coast of China. Obama did not respond. The Chinese, at that point in time, knew that they could take control of many aspects of international policies without opposition. The U.S. influence is contracting at an unimaginable scope.

China has supplied nuclear materials to Pakistan, aided Syria in their quest for nuclear armaments, and has been an advent supporter of North Korea.

The decreasing of military effectiveness easily lends itself to budget cuts in the area of missiles, which are critical in intercepting enemy launches. The only purpose of these actions is to undermine the security of the United

States to such a magnitude that we will be subject to nuclear blackmail. This is a dangerous policy of appeasement.

President Obama is dragging his feet in the matter of Afghanistan while rapidly decreasing our nuclear perceptions and capabilities, and curtailing our missile defense systems. This at a time when exponential nuclear expansion is the radical powers of Iran and North Korea is threatening the globe.

The new nuclear policy of President Obama to reverse a mutually destructive program, serves to motivate those involved in proliferation. Iran, for one, verbally entertained the thought that a nuclear attack on the United States may not invite nuclear retaliation.

An analysis of the hosting of a meeting of the world powers in Washington to promote the recent change in the nuclear plan emphasized the purposeful weakening of the United States. This is an obviously major decision that places the free world in a more perilous dilemma that could result in a nuclear or biological catastrophe. Unequivocally, it invites our enemies to attack. Never before has such a deleterious military decision been made. Thus, we have come full circle of promoting our enemies along with the agenda of Obama. Certain analysis might allude to Obama as being naive in lieu of an intentional perverted statement of logic. A system put in place, at the start of the cold war of mutually assured destruction, provided peace. The empirical evidence is overwhelming, in that a nuclear attack would culminate in similar nuclear response. Now this peacekeeping nuclear doctrine has been abandoned. What is the purpose of this insane illusion?

Charles Krauthammer, a columnist for the Washington Post Writers Group, writing in the Kansas City Star (April 15, 2010), titled, Disaster in The Making, Obama's Nuclear Shift Invites Proliferation. Krauthammer calls it morally bizarre.

"Does anyone believe that North Korea or Iran will be more persuaded to abjure nuclear weapons because they could then carry out a biological or chemical attack on the U.S. without fear of nuclear retaliation?"

"The administration's Nuclear Posture Review declares U.S. determination to continue to reduce the role of nuclear weapons in deterring non-nuclear attacks. The ultimate aim is a blanket doctrine of no first use."

"There can be no greater spur to hyper-proliferation that the furling of the American nuclear umbrella."

Obama in a speech before the 2010 graduating class at West Point prom-ulgated his policy of a new international order to resolve the challenges of our times. The commencement speech focused on turning our security over to global entities. To quote:

"Countering violent extremism and insurgency; stopping the spread of nuclear weapons and securing nuclear materials; combating a changing climate And sustaining global growth; helping countries feed themselves and care for the sick; preventing conflict and heal-ing its wounds".

Everything imaginable is tossed into the mix. The objectives have a nice sound: however they are in the realm of unworkable idealism. It lacks any cohe-sion on the part of any of the world's nations. It has not worked in the past, and since nothing depicting positive actions has emanated, one can only remain skeptical and aware that global alliances have a high degree of failure. How can the United States take such a risk with the negative elements confront-ing us? United States leadership is decimated into oblivion. The international forces, a part of the one world government, are destined to fail. Nowhere is any sort of cooperation shown on the horizon. It is a one sided speech, that when analyzed, shows the U.S. as a marginalized state. It takes on added impe-tus when light is made that the speech is delivered at a U.S. Military Academy.

Another action that should energize our enemies and enervate the U.S. is the inculcation of homosexuality into the military. Here is a large example of the programs devised to uncut the effectiveness of the military mission. The results are cataclysmic.

1. Difficulty in recruiting.
2. Career personnel leaving the military to pursue other careers.
3. Create divisions with the ranks by undercutting the leaders.

Again citing Charles Krauthammer, (Kansas City Star, July 13, 2010), in his writing about a different group of subjects that culminate in identifying the unfavorable personality (or character), of President Obama as a narcissist.

"Obama habitually refers to Cabinet members and other high gov-ernment officials as 'my'-'my secretary of homeland security' 'my national security team,' 'my ambassador.' It's a stylistic detail, but quite revealing of Obama's view of himself."

Charles Krauthammer draws contrasts at the other end of the spectrum, which is modesty.

"Take human rights. After Obama's meeting with the president of Kazakhstan, Mike McFaul of the National Security Council reported that Obama actually explained to the leader of that thuggish plutocracy that we too are working on perfecting our own democracy."

"Nor is this only example of an implied moral equivalence that diminishes and devalues America. Assistant Secretary of State Michael Posner reported that in discussions with China about human rights, the U.S. side brought up Arizona's immigration law - 'early and often.' As if there is the remotest connection between that and the persecution of dissidents, jailing of opponents, suppression of religion routinely practiced by the Chinese dictatorship."

"Nothing new here. In his major addresses, Obama's modesty about his own country has been repeatedly on display as, in one venue after another, he has gratuitously confessed America's alleged failing-from disrespecting foreigners to having lost its way morally after 9/11."

"It's fine to recognize the achievements of other and be non-chauvinistic about one's country. But Obama's modesty is curiously selective. When it comes to himself, modesty is in short supply."

Charles Bolden, Administrator of NASA, was told by Obama to reach out to the Muslim world and help them to feel good about their scientific, math and engineering achievement. Of course they haven't had any in over a thousand years. Also, Bolden set forth the message that Russia was instrumental in making a major contribution to the space station. Krauthammer points out the fervent fact that this supposed achievement took place at a time when the Russian space program fell apart. The U.S. acquired the burden of having to fund the entire space station. Coupled with this is Bolden's statement that the U.S. cannot get to Mars without international assistance. Revamping history and depriving it of its realism and then citing unrealistic circumstances, serve to dwarf the person involved in these inexactitudes.

Here we have identified Obama as being modest on an international scale and narcissistic on a personal scale. Internationally, he continually apologized for us as he aligns with dictators, such as Hugo Chavez, who hate the United States.

A Mars comment- the technology to go to Mars exists; however we do not have the capability of placing a human being on Mars. Obviously, the international community cannot contribute anything in the way of solving this problem. Thus, the statement made by Bolden is false and is part of the program to promote the U.S. as a weak nemesis. Bolden fails to divulge NASA as a shell of its former self.

Obama's space program seems to be in his head. He expresses plans to have astronauts visit an asteroid by 2025. He expects to be alive to see a Mars landing. In a speech at NASA's Kennedy Space Center, Obama exclaimed that he is committed to the manned space program; however we have to do it in a smart way. Of course he is ending the Constellation program. The funding for the space shuttle has been scuttled. The space program is being destroyed. The people working on the project will be fired. Here again is the inverted talk. Our technology development will be curtailed out into the indefinite future. NASA has a track record of providing the private sector and foreign interests with economically feasible technologies. These profitable operations contribute to our internal growth and trade balances. If we cease to operation technologically, all of this is for naught.

CHAPTER 13

STOCKS BONDS RETIREMENT INVESTMENTS

Runaway deficits are obviously not conducive to the proper function of capitalistic markets.

Much has been made of the Greek crisis. Yet as a percent of Gross National Product GNP), the United States and the United Kingdom are in much worse shape. In the U.S., the national deficits have approached 75 percent of GNP. No country has ever survived this astronomical deficit.

Here are some of the many deceptions which have a negative effect on our investments.

1. Unemployment, as reported, is grossly inaccurate and inadequate. Many part time people are counted as a positive side to employment. It appears as though they are employed full time. The private sector is shedding jobs. Even the massive employment of government workers cannot make up for rising unemployment. When unemployed persons stop seeking jobs and their benefits terminate, they are no longer counted as being unemployed. The data should show that unemployment is in the area of 20 percent. No government tampering with the statistics can cover up this devastating situation.
2. Government deficits are incredibly disguised as capital. An identical stance is taken by the banks that refuse to write off bad or uncollectible loans. These are additional nails in the coffin.
3. The global deceptions, particularly by the Central Bankers, permeate the landscape.
4. The regulators like the Security Exchange Commission (SEC), not only fail us as investors, but actually assist the fraudulent perpetrators. The

Consumer Protection Act permits the SEC to turn down information requests under the Freedom of Information Act. This action qualifies the Securities Exchange Commission as a secret organization. How could another explanation of status exist?

5. Mutual fund debacle which tells us to diversify and stay with the same portfolio, which in the majority of situations is void of any flexibility.

6. The analysts do not appear to possess the necessary element of at least attempting to look through a crystal ball and envision a future. There is only a time to buy (fund the portfolio). Reality is an abstraction. A coupling of reality with projections in lieu of numerous observations should emanate one to not base decisions on past activities. Many mutual funds maintained a practical similarity from 2007 to 2008. It resulted in devastated portfolios as stocks experienced a world wide plunge. Investors were told not to look at their portfolios. The story was that the market would recover. Telling the investor to have faith in the system as to its ability to recover had an influence on investors. Panic selling was averted. The action toward holding for the long run was instilled in the psyche of the investor.

7. Much has been said of diversification. It is not without its merits. Diversification falls short of accomplishing goals. The majority of investors does not have the capability or are not willing to make the effort to evaluate risks. Reliance is placed on brokers or financial advisors.

8. Unwinding of the stock markets requires appropriate responses. The current debacle is different from anything we have ever historically witnessed financial institutions, are in panic mode, and void of an ability to react. The constituency desires (understatement) Government to exercise its power to delve in the crises. However, and tragically, the powers are incapable of formulating a solution to this inexorable problem. In fact any of their proposed action is ill advised. It will only make matters worse.

Comparison to the last depression which lasted to the 1940s is ridiculous. It causes the population to conclude a viable solution on the near horizon. The time range for a positive outlook is not discernable. A light at the end of the tunnel is not visible.

Investors clamor for unrealistic returns. Practically every investor has the trait of not determining a selling strategy. The market works in waves. How can a retirement or educational plan be devised on such speculation? The stock markets volatility is severe in bear markets. Statistically, the rallies often lead to inexact conclusion. The market has been is a sideway pattern for a number of years. No one wants to miss a market upswing. It literally siphons money into the market, generating a continuation of the rally. Then the market turns down. Bear markets are deceiving. Actually the stock market is rational. A sizeable element is psychological, predicated on greed and fear.

The employees of the investment world (Wall Street) lead the public to believe that they should "fund" their plan, or add funds, and hold on, not withstanding the gyrations in the stock market. The supposition is that the market will come back. The current stock market does not project any return to higher levels over any long term period. Investors should probably seek dividend paying stock of viable firms. As a reminder, and not to gyrate toward compassion, note that during the so called great depression, the market lost 80 percent of its value.

Gold and silver are practically conservative investments. This follows that conservative stocks, like so many other investments, have taken a bear market beating. What is an investor to do? Hide their money?

Gold and silver is ordinarily a hedge to inflation currencies. Gold, silver and the stock market moved down in unison during 2008. Hedge funds speculation coupled with a thought toward deflation led to a decrease in the price of both gold and silver. One should not be predisposed to believe that silver and gold compliment each other in their prospective price movements. In the future, the price of silver could easily outpace gold. This is primarily because of its limited supply and its industrial use, regardless of a depression or recession.

China and India look as obvious nations to become the next economic powers. India is a socialistic country that appears to be transitioning itself into a capitalistic state, or at least capitalistic cauterizations. This is inspiring and leaves one optimistic about the future in India. Socialism contains many facets that inhibit economic determinations. Bureaucracies, taxes, and many other government requirements have deleterious effects on progress. Often women are mistreated. The "caste system" divides people via obsolete traditions, which also add to the enigma of moving forward. However, to the casual observer, this is changing. Educated women are being hired into the free market places. The economic growth in India will have a tendency to be slower than in China. However, the markets should depict less volatility. The economic growth should be firm with substantial appreciation.

China is still a communist country subscribing to leftist ideologies which inhibits economic growth. On the surface, there is absolute progression. China has its share of enterprising and hard working people. Somewhere in the near future is the obstacle of diminishing returns. Controlling birth rates, corruption, and a continuing gyration toward an aging population are key elements in in stunting the industrial growth. The one child population control is the big detriment to providing a flexible pool of efficiency required for a viable economy. The magnitude of the poverty problem, although assuaged somewhat by the progressive and dynamic economy and numerous environmental problems contribute to the burdensome elements. Excessive concentration on military development, and real or imagined hostility, and a desire to dominate Taiwan and Japan also serve to retard economic efficiency.

The growth outlook for China looks good. The government owns a substantial amount of Chinese business. In the short run, this should not be a problem. China is not likely to reverse course, therefore the long term outlook is good. However, the stock market should continue to experience volatility. Another staggering problem is the lack of females in the population. Somewhere, in the near future, it will have an extremely negative effect. From the motivational and sociological aspects, males will not envision developing a family. How long can China continue limiting an already existing family to one child? It is a desperate methodology to control population growth.

The Chinese renminbi is chained to the dollar. Europe is China's primary trading partner. China pegged the rate to decrease trading competition. The EURO lost significant value. Thus, Chinese exports are more expensive for Europeans. Because of the dollar's rise, many Chinese factories will go out of business. The pegged rate is backfiring. The Chinese also lost when the government purchased EUROS to offset the problems associated with the U.S. Department of the Treasury printing a plethora of dollars.

Certain financial advisors should find another field of work. They become an impediment to the saver or investor keeping their wealth, let alone increase their invested capitol. Specific incidences come to mind. During the market fall in early 2009, financial planners told their clients to not look at the results. The thought was that the market will turn around. It did happen, but for how long will the market stay at its current level. Market timing is difficult. However, the alternative to buying and selling is to take on sizable risk. One must be aware of this. Too many financial planners and analysts hold out that they know in which direction the market is heading. As one may determine, the crystal ball is not always clear enough to provide a profit. There are, for example, mutual fund managers that are emulated for bringing in sizeable profits. One such analyst gained 40% in less that a year. He was practically immortalized. A short time later, the stock market turned south. The result was a loss that was greater than the 40%.

One has to be a knowledgeable investor. It requires work and does not assure success. But it does accomplish the task of recognition of the risk.

Persons on retirement or planning to join the retiree status, have to plan so called conservative investments. Since the government has tampered with interest rates to such a magnitude as to bring interest rates close to or at zero. This takes money out of the pockets of purchasers of these "sick" interest instruments. It also causes persons seeking a reasonable rate of return, to make investments that could be deemed speculative. Specifically, with interest on many instruments being close to a zero, many feel compelled to invest in common stocks. This moves the price of equities higher and thereby subjected to higher sell offs. The market downside is called a correction. It assumes by definition that the market did something wrong, and is therefore obligated to correct.

In October of 2008, the stock and bond markets experienced a terrible sell off, creating a problem of crises proportions. It extended into the banking system. Investors and speculators experiences margin calls. They have to sell stocks and bonds to cover their loans. This also included the hedge funds. It left a world wide gaping whole. However, the market sustained itself. Although in October it did not return to a full recovery position, the data clearly indicated that the stock and bond markets and the banks would still operate in a viable fashion. This is important, because a short time later, the news was reporting that the bank system was on the brink of failure. Congress did not believe this. The legislatures voted against the TARP funds. It was the new day that the brow beating and propaganda machines went into full swing. Wolf Blitzer of CNN was exclaiming the catastrophes extending to small business as they were unable to meet payroll. Nowhere did anyone mention a specific business. It was all a deploy and part of a concerted effort, extending to the Bush White House, aimed at Congress to go back and vote for the TARP funds. Thus, anytime there is a chasm between the banking interests and taxpayers, the taxpayers will loose. Over the next couple of years, the citizens were told that the TAPR funds saved the economy by saving the banks, which were on the verge of collapse. Even if they were, wouldn't it be better for some of these banks to fail. The discussion also involves brokerage houses insurance companies. Many of them were able to pay out billions of dollars to a selected few. If the TARP money was instead, properly, placed into the economy it could have created and infinite number of jobs.

Many different types of investments need to be considered. Metals, commodities, real estate, bonds, stocks should be major considerations in a decent portfolio. One may diversify, internationally, throughout this spectrum; however, each aspect must be adequately researched and analyzed. The current state of affairs seems to favor gold, silver, commodities and rare metals. China and India, as expanding economies, are consuming these resources. Silver should outperform gold. Also, during the 1930 depression, the government confiscated gold. Rare metals are becoming rarer and, accordingly, are increasing in value. These metals have a variety of uses, such as electronics, and nuclear energy. Many of these are vital for our defense. The developed world is aware of these metals being vital for many domestic needs. China possesses many of these rare metals. It has already begun to restrict export of some of its rare metals.

With the ability of government and others to manipulate markets, investments in minerals have to be closely observed by the small speculators.

Recent meetings by key Democrats, mostly clandestine, centered on another serious take away program. The future legislation would be tantamount to confiscation of your retirment funds. The title would probably be, the Guaranteed Retirement Fund. The government would take over these trillions of dollars and dole them out as it seems fit. This is going on in Hungary. Argentina successfully accomplished this demonic action. There is too much money for the secular progressives to leave on the table, so to speak. Somehow they believe this is their money. The union pension funds would, under the program, receive a large amount of your money. Why are these grotesque measures being discussed? It is because they can avail themselves of your funds and hand them out to a favorable group of Democratic voters. The union pension funds have been used for political donations to the Democratic Party. The unions simply do not have the ability to make good on the pension promises. So now we have future proposals designed to be placed on top of the Social Security system. Note than a special commission has already recommended that an individual desiring to collect on the social security money that he or she contributed into the system, must wait until age 69. Of course it doesn't take much mathematical ability to conclude that a vast portion of the population will not live long enough to collect on the government's promise.

Again, there is another demovtivator in the works to undermine investment, by confiscating hard earned funds.

CHAPTER 14

TAXES

The federal income tax system is used as a political tug of war. The Bush tax cuts decreased taxes to the middle class and provided significant increases to the lower and middle class via child tax credits and earned income credits. A sizeable portion of these dollars ended up in the hands of illegal aliens.

We are incessantly told that the upper class enjoys lower tax rates. Really! The upper class pays a sizeable portion of income taxes. At least fifty percent of the income is surrendered in taxes and this is only the federal income tax. Sixty percent of the legal population pay less than one percent of the income taxes. Therefore, the liability of paying over 99 percent of the income taxes falls to forty percent of the legal population. This is magnified by the people who receive many dollars characterized by tax credits, for example, the child care credit and the Earned Income Credit. Translated, a statistically significant number of these people not only do not pay any income taxes, but receive cash credits. This relief program within the IRS culminates in billions of handed out dollars. Many persons adjust their earnings to receive close to the maximum credits.

Increasing tax rates results in less revenues. It is consistently happening. The economy deteriorates accordingly, and results in fewer earnings. Additionally, those targeted members of the populous find a method to pay fewer taxes.

In Maryland, the liberal legislature raised the taxes on the so called rich. After the cheering and returning to reality, the million of dollars the liberals counted on actually resulted in a tragic loss of billions of dollars. The rich moved their wealth where it would be treated better. Many also moved themselves, thus eliminating a significant tax base.

Kansas almost passed similar catastrophic legislation. Kansas cannot be ruled out as a future developer of this program. Already, a city in Kansas is taxing individuals and businesses on the use of their driveways. It is analogous to a toll road right outside your front door.

Out of desperation to fund the supposedly necessary elements of the budget, many states have raised or are on the verge of raising taxes. The negative consequences are incalculable.

The columnist, George Will, writing in April 2010, in the Kansas City Star, explained the tragic results of increasing taxes on the wealthy and the dilemma faced by the newly elected Governor of New Jersey-Chris Christie.

"He inherited a $2.2 billion deficit, and next year's projected deficit of $10.7 billion, is relative to the state's $29.3 billion budget, the nation's worst. Democrats, with the verbal tic - 'Tax the rich!' - that passes for progressive thinking, demanded that he reinstate the 'millionaires tax' which hit millionaires earning $400,000 until it expired Dec.31. Christie noted that between 2004 and 2008 there was a net outflow of $70 billion in wealth as 'the rich' including small businesses, fled. And the previous administrations had raised taxes 115 times in the last eight years alone."

"Challenging teachers unions to live up to their cloying 'it's really about the kids' rhetoric, he has told them to choose between a pay freeze and job cuts. Validating his criticism, some Bergen County teachers encouraged student, to cut classes and go to the football field to protest his policies. Christie notes that the $550,000 salary of the executive director of the teachers union is larger than the total cuts proposed for 190 of the state's 605 school districts."

"Christie is reminding New Jersey that wealth goes where it is welcome and stays where it is well treated."

George Will goes on to point out:

1. The retirement plan of police officers, among the nations highest paid, who can retire after 25 years of public service at a rate of 65 percent of their highest salary.
2. Sixty six percent of public employees are unionized. Unionized workers can buy officials with taxpayer money.

There are items here which need to be emphasized. Unions are able to spend vast sums of the taxpayer dollars to influence government actions. The union also uses the vile tactic of intimidation. It is for this one reason alone that the secret ballot should be retained. In other words employees in voting to join or not to join a union should be on a secretive ballot and not open to the seeing eyes of union officers. This is called the ballot initiative.

Retirement requirements for civil service employees are increasingly consuming a larger part of the budget. Even at current levels it is becoming impossible for state governments to cough up the funds. Promises were made in the past when it appeared ideal for politicians to receive credit for adopting these generous programs. The day of reckoning approaches and there is not a formidable solution. It becomes apparent that the politicians are void of an ability to act upon a problem that they or their predecessors created.

Many union retirees receive medical compensation. In some states, like California, the problem is invasive, perhaps 60 % of budget. It cannot be paid for by the current tax collections. It is an element contributing to the bankruptcy of the state system. The federal government is in a constant process of increasing taxes to provide a framework for this out of control taking of the public purse.

Numerous states are or will be facing this retirement funding problem. Unfunded retirement programs in many of the private sector entities are faced with the identical problem. In the public sector the politicians, unable to cut back on expenditures, will resort to raising taxes. This will further motivate people to take means to avoid the imposition. Like in California, and Maryland, the wealth and eventually the rich members, domiciled in the states, will seek a locale where they are welcomed. The preceding is not an eventuality, it is now occurring. Many people are sending their capital overseas. More of the nation's wealth is leaving the country.

The tax codes are a complicated mess. It is an example of government's lack of competency. Complications are developed by Government to confuse the population. How can you explain a tax code that no one understands? It becomes another method of non arguable tax collection. Because high tax rates, for the so called rich existed in the past, is not justification for future high rates.

The Obama Administration is rapidly attempting to remove the mobility of wealth out of the country. At the onset it appeared to attack only

Switzerland by requesting confidential information on American citizens. The Obama bullying mechanism portrayed its methodology by threatening the Swiss banks with gigantic fines. The Swiss banking system would have to compromise their secrecy laws to comply with this grotesque request. It is not a matter of presenting the case as a noble attempt directed at collecting taxes, due and payable by the wealthy. Instead it presupposes that we cannot tolerate and therefore must terminate the ability of countries to determine how to best run their banking systems.

Many times throughout its history, Switzerland has been under the gun to provide what they consider confidential and secretive information to the prying eyes of foreign governments. The Nazis, for example, wanted to know if an individual had an account. They did not pry to know how much. That was a separate issue. The information would be disclosed by the person having such an account.

All of this presents an enigma for the Swiss. They feel forced to take action. In the instant case, an American is precluded from opening account in Switzerland, without meeting exasperating conditions. The end result is an arrant depiction of the desire of the Swiss not to do business with Americans. This has a sizeable economic negative impact, which extends to other sovereigns. Thus, Americans are singled out to climb obstacles in order to compete. This is because the compliance of tax matters cannot be remedied domestically.

The projection is for the Internal Revenue Service to use whatever tactic they can get away with to achieve the goal of harassing U.S. citizens. In October of 2009, the IRS established a multi person task force to achieve this goal. From the handwriting on the wall, this will apply to citizens and expatriates-specifically American Citizens living in foreign countries. Already there are regulations being written to extend the reach of the U.S. government to confiscate a percentage of the wealth of these people. So the changes in the tax mechanism are not limited to the rich. It will extend the complicated method and language of the tax system to operating outside the United States. American citizens as a protective device may resort to relinquishing their citizenship.

As of end of 2009, approximately one half of our workers do not pay any income tax. Of these, fully 40% receive dollars, in some form, from the government, such as an earned income credit or a child care credit. Nowhere do you vision these as welfare programs. And yes, it extends to illegal persons.

Take a look at this partial tax list:

accountants receivables	building permit	cigarettes
Personal income	dog licenses	excise
unemployment	food licenses	fuel
gross receipts	inventories	liquor
luxury	property	real estate
service charges	social security	automobiles
road usage	school	state income
state unemployment	telephone	utilities
watercraft	well permit	corporate income

Now there are proposals to tax:

air as in carbon   a value added tax   tax on drive way use

These taxes did not exist, and our nation was the most prosperous in the world. We had no national debt, had the largest middle class in the world, and Mom stayed home to raise the children.

Not too long ago, married women worked to supplement the family income. In many cases it determined the standard of the vacation. Later as taxes increasingly consumed the family income, the wife was working to help pay the taxes.

As a side note, we are aware that women are a vital part of our economy. This is not part of the argument. However, the disintegration of the family is absolutely in question.

CHAPTER 15

INTERNATIONAL II

PALESTINE- THE NON EXISTENT STATE.

Israel is fighting for their lives (survival). By the middle of 2010, Israel appears to be standing alone. It is as though Obama has pulled the rug out from under our allies. The press is against Israel and is in favor of terrorism. It is gratifying (to them) to report the loss of civilian life on the Hamas side of the war. What about the Israelites who suffer from the Hamas rockets? Is this not news? Purposeful distortions and obvious lack of knowledge create this diabolical reporting. What about Hamas torturing the Palestinians in Gaza? Yet our government, at the introduction of the Obama Administration, has provided the terrorists with billions of dollars. How can our representative even consider such outrageous handouts or are they just plain impudent? This amount of funds, if used properly, could create a large number of jobs here in the United States.

Israel plays a vital part in our quest to subdue terrorism. The Obama apparent desertion of Israel is having negatively profound ramifications. The United States is perceived as not having a validation of our international allies.

SOUTH KOREA ı JAPAN

South Korea and Japan, are closely watching the Obama administration. Already the Prime Minister of Japan, the United States educated Hatoyama, has had to resign over the dispute in Okinawa. In seeking election, Hatoyama promised to close U.S. military facilities in Okinawa. The people of Okinawa want the U.S. to close the Marine base at Futenma and the air force base at Kadena. It is a strange occurrence with the Marines, as they were to move to Guam and the air base at Kadena was to remain operational. The inhabitants of Okinawa want the valuable land for their economic use. The U.S. is able to influence, for the time being, the retention of the air base at Kadena, but this does not extend to the Japanese people continuing their acceptance of the U.S. to the degree of precluding the resignation of Hatoyama. Two possible conclusions exist on this matter. One is the manner in which the Toyota executive was treated by members of congress (impolitely) over the subject of the recent recall of Toyota automobiles for safety reasons, and secondly, the absolute inaction to the indiscriminate North Korean firing of missiles over the territory of Japan. Japan, is a vital participant, in our war against terror. Apparently, at this moment, they may have determined that as far as defense is concerned, they are on there own.

PALESTINE : ISRAEL

The Obama regime is attempting diplomacy with Hamas. What can develop - a partnership with terrorists? Imagine having diplomatic relationships with Abbas. He is not really in control of anything. Some of his terrorist's troops walk around the Palestinian city of Ramallah. So why does Abbas get money from us? What about diplomacy with the terrorist state of Syria? Providing importance to Syria or Iran via diplomacy is extremely counter productive. These two states are busy developing nuclear weapons. Syria obtained quite a portion of their nuclear capability from Iraq. Much of this was destroyed by an Israeli air raid.

In June of 2010, Obama provided four hundred million dollars to the Palestinian cause. This is in addition to an obscene amount of close to one billion dollars for Gaza (Hammas) when he first became President. The purpose was to bolster Obama's standing in the Arab world. Note the negativism that this generates for us Americans and our friends around the world. Here is another action viewed as a weakness. What else could possibly be the purpose of this action?

Three items to consider:
1. The United States does not have the money.
2. Money is needed for domestic use.
3. The current budget is out of control -an understatement.

The Middle East policy has not varied by many degrees since 1947. It has been constant failure, characterized by grasping at the United Nations for solutions. The UN has a suppress Israel agenda. Obama has a suppress Israel attitude. The most drastic is to appease Iran, in particular, even though they are developing nuclear weapons and have directly threatened Israel with annihilation. Passive speeches and denouncing the United States as was done, for example, in Cairo lends itself to embolden the terrorist enemies. Oslo secret peace talks took place over 16 years ago. The United States has sunk billions of dollars into the Palestinians organizations. Instead of developing a peace initiative, they enslaved the very people they were to help develop their hopes. The Arafat group prohibited the institutions from improving Arab life. The miserable life was said to be the fault of Israel. Schools, roads and hospitals were not built. Hate is still being expressed as a major part of the school curriculum. There is still an ongoing war between the terrorist factions - Hamas and Al Fatah. Hamas took over control in Gaza. They destroyed Arab houses under the guise of using the land to build high rises. These stately buildings never rose. Further methods to make sure life is miserable in Palestine.

By June of 2010, certain elements of the world, prompted by the United Nations, embarked on a program to challenge Israel's blockade of Gaza. The blockade has only one purpose that is to keep war materials out of the hands of terrorists and consequently offset the shelling of rockets into Israel. Hamas sought to enhance the anti Israeli impetus by not accepting the so called humanitarian aid. Certainly they did not think that would go anywhere.

Turkey, a past friend of Israel, was selected to develop a flotilla to challenge the blockade of Gaza. A case could easily be made for the complicity of the Obama administration in the formulation of a flotilla.

To the untrained eye, it appears as though a peace treaty was eminent. It grew out of the secret Norway conferences. Nowhere did the Norway Accords have any possibility of success. The Clinton administration sent many dollars to Yassar Arafat. In the end the peace treaty fell apart and the terrorist, Yassar Arafat, became rich. As part of the peace talks, the indigenous Arabs sought to acquire the right of return to Israel. Jerusalem and the right of return were not then, nor is it now endowed with a possibility of compromise. It would terminate the existence of Israel.

In actuality, this is one element of the worldwide war generated by the Islamic terrorists.

Israel is in a constant state of war against the terrorists occupiers of Gaza. Therefore, according to international law, the blockade is legal. Israel should never have departed Gaza. The plan was to trade land for peace. It turned out to be a tragic action. It not only affected Israelis, but the Palestinians who were deprived of their freedoms and experienced a lowering of their standard of living by the corrupt Mahmoud Abbas regime and later Hamas. Over 4000 rockets were fired into Israel from Gaza. At one point the Israelis went on a war footing and launched an invasion of Gaza. This happened in December of 2008. Israel in fighting for its survival inhibited the rocket fire. This can only be recognized as a short term solution. The world community instead of reaching a consensus of opinion, to have Hamas ceases their action against Israel accused Israel of what is tantamount to genocide.

On September 22, 2009, coincidently during the high Jewish holiday of Rosh Hashanah, a report, called the Goldstone report, was released by the United Nations, excoriating Israel for their invasion of Gaza. Richard Goldstone, a South African judge, is Jewish. He is also an Israeli basher. In short, it is a political attack comprised of 575 pages, directed at demonizing Israel. It blocked the facts (truth) behind the Gaza war. Perhaps Goldstone is promulgating himself into a UN promotion. There has to be some reason for Goldstone to gyrate into the abyss of the U.N. anti Israel fever.

In an article on September 18, 2009 in the Jerusalem Post, Goldstone stated:

"Israel must investigate and Hamas is obliged to do the same. They must examine what happened and appropriately punish any soldier or commander found to have violated the law".

It obviated the obvious that in the invasion into Gaza, Israel went to extremes to protect civilian lives. General Gabi Ashkenazi called the Goldstone report biased and unbalanced. He pointed out that Hamas would not engage in open field. Hamas hid among the civilians, like women and children. Israel used the media and other communication methods to warn the civilian population. This action within itself, helped eliminate many civilian casualties. Nowhere in the report can it be found that the Israeli civilian population was subjected to missal attacks from Gaza into Israel. A couple of days after the report, Hamas Prime Minister, Ismail Haniyeh, recommended that the U.N. bring the Israel criminals to justice. Nothing was heard from the Obama administration.

The methodology of the report was faulty. The U.N. commission failed to look into the actions of Hamas, before and during the war, such as the indiscriminate firing of motor shells into Palestinian and Israel neighborhoods, resulting in civilian casualties.

During the December 2008 war, CNN reported along with other left wing news organizations, that Israel was the aggressor. The propaganda disseminated from the news organizations, characterized Hamas as having 15,000 plus warriors alerted and ready to combat the Israel Defense Forces (IDF). Coupled with this was their in the field reporters depicting explosions as having come from mines placed by Hamas. Here we have distorted and contrived news accounts as to the effectiveness of Hamas in the battlefield. The explosions were in fact the Israel Air Force hitting their designated targets, such as ammunition storage facilities. Within days the invading force prevailed, depicting Hamas as a weak, ragged and ineffective force.

Caroline B. Glick in the September 18, 2009 edition of the Jerusalem Post wrote, Our Irredeemable International System. It outlines the foreign policy of the United States, particularly in relation to the Middle East and the United Nations. It is a straightforward editorial.

"Unlike Bush, Obama has enthusiastically embraced the notion that the UN should by right have a leading role in international affairs. He also accepted the UN's basic notion that the interest of world peace, the US and its democratic allies should bow to the desires of despots and dictators."

"So it is this week he abandoned US allies Poland and the Czech Republic in his bid to appease Russia. So it is that his administration has sided with ousted Honduran president Manuel Zalaya, who, with the support of Venezuelan dictator Hugo Chavez, sought to undermine Honduran democracy against the lawful government and democratic defenders. So it is that the administration has sided with the genocidal mullahs in Teheran over their democratic opponents. So it is that the administration has adopted the view that Israel is to blame for the absence of peace in the Middle East and embraced as legitimate political actor's Palestinian terror groups that refuse to accept Israel's right to exist."

Within the time frame of nine months into the Obama Presidency, the upheaval became globally evident. With Obama taking such a passive stance in crucial situations against dictatorships, it places the UN and the dictators in control of the destiny of the US. This undermining is a far fetched statement; however, all these negative elements are true.

CIA has a high probability of spite work resulting in reliance on other countries to furnish Intelligence. At best it is animosity directed toward President George W. Bush and is more likely controlled by various people at the top, who were determined to see a failure of the administration. This has more importance than protecting the United States. Recruitment and training of people to be fluent in the local languages, in which they must operate, is nonexistent. The usefulness of the information must be correlated and specific determinations made. Organizational operations of this type undermine the security of the United States. Gratitude's need to be extended to those persons in the CIA who excel at their work to protect us citizens and are fortunately self motivated to perform their tasks - even to their risking of lives.

Iran is on the verge of completing development of nuclear weapons. Here we have a terrorist state with a top agenda to become a member of the nuclear club. Can Syria be far behind? Are they not the beneficiary of Iraq's atomic program? The program formulated to attempt to solve this enigma is to pursue vigorous diplomacy. Thus, credibility is given to these international outlaws.

The mujahideen are increasing their presence and influence in Indonesia. The mujahideen council led by Syawal Yasin, an Al-Quida trainee on the Pakistan - Afghanistan border is seen as a method to place impetus on the handling of the Islamic terrorist agenda. He is in fact the son-in-law of the founder of an Indonesian terrorist group.

The extreme radical terrorists look upon this method as a weakness. Also it gives them prominence in lieu of obscurity. It cannot possibly have anything but a deleterious effect. Terrorist states cannot be assuaged. Iran views itself as an entity out in front of the Islamic world with its nuclear endeavors.

Recent successful terrorist activities can only motivate the enemy. We have an administration that is impervious to reality. The world doesn't stop because the President decides to take a vacation. Simply, days off do not come with the territory. All of this highlights the incompetence of the administration. Characterized by the ineptness of staff sitting in Washington to take care of the "happenings", one cannot but wonder if they are even concerned with anything outside their agenda. A competent executive has things arranged so that if the seat is vacant for a few days, the staff can perform efficiently. Here we have a tragic case of incompetence.

In considering two cases, Dr. Nidal Hasan, Major U.S. Army, and Umar Farouk Abdulmutallab, a 23year old terrorist, one can only conclude that Homeland Security and the White House were totally unprepared to deal with the these terrorist acts. In fact they did not even conclude that they were acts of terrorists. Obama at the onset of the Detroit incident called Abdulmutallab a suspect and falsely stated that he acted alone. This obvious attempt to minimize the situation was a dynamic change of tone. Its goal, which backfired, did not serve to undermine the severity of the incident? Immediately becoming embarrassing are the lies which are set forth to garner credibility. There is no hole, big enough, even in Hawaii, where the President could hide. President Obama's response to the Nidal Hasan massacre was "not to jump to conclusion".

On Christmas day we experienced a terrorist attack that, fortunately, did not go off as planned. Abdulmutallab should change the perception that some have inaccurately portrayed, that terrorism rises out of poverty and despair. Abdulmutallab was an engineer who came from a family of means. He was said to be depressed and lonely. Can we develop a picture of him being the victim?

A case at practically the same time showed the destructive capability of Al Quida. An explosion by a suicidal Jordanian doctor in Afghanistan, who was not to be outdone by Abdulmuttalab, killed a high number of CIA agents. He was supposedly a double agent super spy. Again a lapse of security showed its ugly head.

Dr. Nidal Hasan, the Psychiatrist, kills a number of our soldiers at Fort Hood. Obama makes a speech telling us not to jump to conclusions - like he isn't a terrorist. Here, again, we approach the question of not facing reality. The administration repeated the scenario in the case of Uram Farouk Adbulmutallab. The administration showed a vast element of being unprepared. The world was shocked at this incompetence. The follow up was deplorable. The President looked perplexed and incompetent. Coupled with this is a gigantic staffing problem. His Homeland Security Chief, Janet Napolitano, lurked into the spotlight to make the declarative statement that the system worked. This immediately signed a complete breakdown with reality. This by a person already known to be outspoken in the wrong direction and promoting open borders. As Governor of New Mexico she was more than animated on the fixation of generating border traffic - bringing the travelers into the country. It was the same Janet Napolatano that in addressing terrorism pointed a finger at our returning military troops. The essence of the message was to keep an eye on them. How secure can this Secretary of Homeland Security make you feel?

Defending her was the President's Chief of Staff on National Security; this was the person who stated that there was no smoking gun in the Uram Farouk Abdulmutallab. He also told us via the major news networks that there were "no smoking guns". It was easy to count five.

The culture of political correctness is devastating. Look at the information what was bottled up in the Nidal Hasan case.

Due process was extended automatically to Abdulmutallab. Was there something behind this that can, at this juncture, only be imagined? Perhaps a lawyer needed to be immediately provided to shut him up. It doesn't take much of an attempt to grasp the facts and to question such a bold maneuver.

The plan of action started to take place after January 1, 2010. O'Bama back from vacation, along with many members of his staff decided on a course of rhetoric to make us believe that they are on top of the terrorist situation. Apparently by this stage of his Presidency very few believe him. His popularity has shrunk along with his credibility. Overseas, he is a laughing stock. No doubt, Al Quida has carefully measured the speeches and actions and found this aid and comfort incredibly perplexing.

Obama's speech stated that we will do whatever it takes to defeat them. A stunning mendacious statement given the penchant Obama has to:

1. Provide due process to non-citizen terrorists
2. Extending Constitutional rights to non-citizen terrorists.
3. Prepare for trials in New York of the vilest terrorists.
4. Have the assistance of the Justice Department in carrying out these bazaar objectives.
5. Have the Justice Department work against the CIA. There is such a restriction on interrogation that much of the gathered intelligence is worthless. There is no suggestion of torture. This is a term used by the radical left to preclude the questioning of terrorists.
6. Release terrorists from Guantanamo. Many were scheduled to be returned to Yemen.
7. Do not recognize terrorists as terrorists. How about suspects?

For us citizens, there are the increasingly ridiculous hurdles at the Airport. Billions more will be spent by these incompetents to reign more restrictions upon us.

Another statement Obama made since returning from his Christmas vacation alluded to Guantanamo as a helpful source of recruitment for Al-Quida. Obama, "make no mistake about it, Guantanamo will be closed." A major favor to the radical left. It will affect our national security. If fact it already has. President Obama refused, until January 2010, to admit that we are at war with al-Qaida. Denying the existence of jihad is not longer an option for the administration. It focuses a spotlight on an obvious disassociation with reality.

The administration has many inexperienced radicals that have nothing but contempt for us citizens. Their statements and actions are unmistakable. Being at war places us in a more perilous situation. The U.S. is not going out to destroy the enemy. The rules of engagement place the military at too much risk and prohibit it from completing what should be its mission.

Taking the troops out of Afghanistan prior to victory is obviously not a plan to win a war. Naturally the American people are against troop deployment. What is the purpose if the plan isn't to win the war? This is another element of incredibility and persuasiveness in an incompetent administration. One still has to connect the political dots to attempt to make a determination if this incompetence is not predicated on a purposeful policy.

The Intelligence Community Security people were so void of capability; it may prompt some to intimate that it was spite work to undermine President Obama. As an afterthought these same people attempted to blame the Bush administration. Since they initiated the system they should be responsible for its shortcomings. What Obama people undisguised in their ignorance and incompetence? All of this is occurring without any sign of positive change.

The political analyst, Dick Morris, does not hesitate to tell us what is happening with our national security:

"Obama has the hunters hunted. The intelligence officers that are supposed to find terrorists are themselves being subjected to the likes of Eric Holder and to criticism within the United States. The administration has discouraged CIA officers from taking the initiative leaps of judgment needed to connect the dots and prevent terrorists from striking the United States."
"So when Obama says it's a systematic failure, yeah it is. But it is one that he caused by the policies that he's has been espousing. It's the logical consequence of all the things he's said ever since he started to run for president".

This was in an interview with Newsmax.com on January 9, 2010.

Dick Morris also went on to add his projection of the vast amount of losses in the November elections for the Democrats. To many, The Obamas "yes we can" now means business as usual. How quaint, given the propensity to obviate any progress on our behalf. The momentum to undermine the United States at every turn appears to be an unrelenting goal. Which brings out the question - given his inexperience, incompetence, and his surrounding himself with people that are not only incompetent, but also lack the direction outside of sycophantic politics?

The Department of Homeland Security is in the throes of building its permanent home on 200 acres in Washington D.C. For starters, it will provide for 25000 employees. Homeland Security has another opportunity to spend vast amounts of money, supposedly for our national security. This is an example of empire building at its worse. Appropriately, this megatropolis is being constructed on the old site of St. Elizabeth's Hospital. This federal hospital was formerly for the insane.

Homeland Security should never have been formed; it is yet another example of improperly functioning organization that is in a critical area of operations. Its personnel are precluded by policies from acting on our behalf. In addition it is too big and cumbersome. The 9/11 commission strongly recommended the formulation of the institution. Perhaps logically they could not envision it being run by incompetents and those who do not have the interests of the United States in the forefront. Homeland Security was created under the pretense that the various agencies were not sharing security information. Now it is worse. Instead of having the authority for action, the information is required to be passed along to other organizations within Homeland Security for action. The more people who are involved increase the chances of the information not being acted upon. After all, you are in a state of polarization if you are unable to connect the dots. Initiative and action are more remote.

President Obama stated that he is the one responsible for all of this tragedy. He assumed the blame, as he said, "the buck stops here." What does this mean? He isn't going to resign or make the situation better by staffing with competent people, and let them identify the problem and take action.

The Enemy Within, by Michael Savage, expounds upon the enemy segment of Islam and the "pass" they are acquiring from the Left.

"In a twisted way, it's because the Dogs of Hate hope to see Islam spread in America in order to overcome the hated Christian white male. You don't understand the psychology of these people. You haven't any idea how sick and demented and dangerous they really are."

"I warn you, don't underestimate your enemy".

"There are jihads in Afghanistan, Bosnia, Chechnya, Cyprus, East Timor, Indonesia, Kashmir, Kosovo, Kurdistan, Macedonia, the Middle East, Nigeria, the Philippines, the Sudan, and Uganda. Fifteen conflicts with one common denominator. All involve Muslims who can't get along with their neighbors".

"Anis Shorrosh, an Arab-American convert to Christianity and author of two books, reported on a secret Islamic twenty year plan to bring America to her knees".

Anis Shorrosh in his book. Islam: A Threat or a Challenge, actually itemized the following:

1. Through sizable grants, the Muslim invaders would create "Centers for Islamic Studies" at the major universities and colleges.
2. Open "front" charities in the United States who ultimately funnel American dollars to support Islamic terror activity.
3. Encourage mass immigration of Muslims, which has averaged more that a hundred thousand annually in since the sixties. Then, teach them to have as many children as possible since all children automatically and irrevocably become Muslims.
4. Manipulate the intelligence agencies (FBI, CIA) with false and misleading reports of terrorism to elevate a sense of vulnerability and strike fear in the hearts of Americans.
5. Use all possible channels of propaganda to convince the American's that terrorists have co-opted Islam when, in reality, the opposite is true. Islam has hijacked the terrorists for their purposes.

Our President Obama, while on one of his out of the country jaunts, proclaimed that the United States is a Muslim nation. In at least one of his domestic speeches, he subverted that fact that we are an extension of the Judean Christian ethic. He mentioned a plethora of religions including Buddhism as if they were part of the founding and moral codes of the United States. Another example of the bazaar ness inculcated into the administrations distortion of History.

A minimum of 200 million dollars will be the cost for just the New York City show trial. There is not one sane reason to hold these trials outside of

Guantanamo Bay. There are many reasons to have military trials at Guantanamo. Given the federal rules of evidence, the enemy will be provided, via subpoena duces tecum, many of our innermost secrets, which extends to clandestine "persons" who at the risk of their lives, assisted the United States in its pursuit of noble endeavors. Will all of this legal maneuvering result in amnesty?

It might be added that Obama signed, in January 2010, an executive order to declassify millions of documents - all at one sitting. The actual damage will most likely take years to determine. Again, what is the reason for these decisions? The Attorney General Holder also needs to be held accountable for his involvement in this matter.

Attorney General Eric Holder, appearing before the House on March 17, 2010, asserted that Osama Bin Laden will never face trial in the United States because he will never be captured alive. In other words, to be a student of the obvious, he will never be read his Miranda rights. Of course following the irrationality of policies or statements, Khalid Shaikh Mohammed will remain incarcerated even if he is not convicted. Here we have a new stance on perverted justice.

Again striking at the heart of the United States, in New York City, is the desecration of the World Trade Center area by the construction of a Mosque. The start of the project would be on September 11, 2011. Heading up the project is Imam Feisal Abdul Raul, a supporter of terrorists. From where is the funding forthcoming? The Mosque is to serve as a symbol of victory. To the American citizen, it is yet another travesty of 9/11. Mayor Bloomberg agrees with the construction project. Why? There is an abyss between the 9/11 legacy and religious freedom. Iman Raul said that the U.S. is an accessory to 9/11. The disaster was a direct result of policies that according to Raul ended in the deaths of children.

Not to be outdone by the excoriations of Mayor Michael Bloomberg, Thomas Freidman, in a New York Times commentary, quoted Imam Raul as having condemned the actions of 9/11. When could this quote have taken place? Americans are to be applauded because of our interfaith tolerance. (Ref.Kansas City Star, 6 August 2010).

Four days later Mary Sanchez, again in the Kansas City Star, wrote, Proceed with the Mosque and Preserve Freedom.

"There is no better way to show how far the U.S. has come from the pathetically naive days when so many asked, 'Why do they hate us?' We should get it by now. Islamic radicals despite what the U.S. claims to be tolerant, accepting, and big enough for all faiths. This is an opportunity to prove it."

Note how the U.S. was pathetically naive and now has an opportunity to prove who we are - just let the construction begin. Further, refraining from opposing the mosque has some cause and effect correlation to the preservation of our freedom.

To the lock steppers, it is the U.S. which must take the high ground and the initiative of proving how tolerant we are. For a change, wouldn't it be sort of nice if others proved something to us.

She continued to praise Michael Bloomberg as eloquent and realistic: however she cited the absurd notion that separation of church and state exists in this case. Then it becomes convenient to uphold the constitution. The group purposely fails to see the provocation involved in the construction of the mosque. One has to merely ask, what is the reason to construct a mosque in the area of the world trade center?

Originally, the issue was attempted to be portrayed as a local incident. It was a method to circumvent or refrain from making statement, which may support the majority interest or in the alternative, support the minority view. It is a countrywide view. The 9/11 attack was an attack on the U.S.A.

When an individual or group wants to subvert the wishes of the majority, they revert to obsessing over the necessity of casting aside their obstructive thinking and grasping the opportunity to prove something, even though it is against the common grain. Obama has expressed himself in this instance as part of the counter culture. It is against the vast opinion of the citizens. So is this - Imam Raul has accepted a taxpayer funded position at the Department of State as a traveling ambassador to the Middle East.

The President's visit to India comes at a time when he is severely weakened by the election results. Further, his policies and programs have weakened the United States and thereby have made it virtually impossible for him to be effective in his international dealings. Thus, it extends far beyond the November elections. The Times of India, October 22, 2010, cited the visit as an opportunity to give substance to the term "natural allies." India is for all intensive purpose, a socialistic country. However, as is evident, India is rapidly developing and adopting many capitalistic tendencies. No one can argue that they are not a democratic country. India's values, legal system, and ideological philosophies are closely aligned with the U.S. Somehow, the impression is like we are not doing enough for India. The implication in for the U.S. to make commitments directed toward the well being of India. Help is being sought by India with its Kashmir problem. China is interfering in any process to smooth the Kashmir situation. Pakistan appears as having a close relationship with China. Rapprochement by India is limited in scope. Obama is apparently not competent to engage in this complicated process. The Obama image abroad is weakened. China is also mentioned by India as being one of the instigators in Sri Lanka. Nowhere is their any evidence of anyone, other than India, confronting the Chinese on these issues. Are these Chinese actions used to inhibit India's economic growth? The matter is further complicated by the appeasement of Pakistan by the United States, probably secondary to the Afghan war. Nevertheless, the U.S. is providing billions of additional dollars of armaments to Pakistan in an effort to provoke them into taking action against the indigenous terrorists.

India and Pakistan split up. It was during the reign of Ghandi, the peace "people" decided to create the separate state of Pakistan. This was immediately after India gained independence from the British Empire in 1946. Pakistan and India are now nuclear powers. Both have been on a war footing since the breakup. Bangladesh, which was a part of Pakistan, is now an independent state. It serves to point out how difficult it is for people to live together. Had they not bifurcated, and attempted to hash out their problems, internally, many of the current confrontations would not be taking place.

CHAPTER 16

CONCLUSIONS

A government motivated to suppress its inhabitants has specific categories and goals at its disposal.

RESTRICT GUNS
RESTRICT EXITING OF CURRENCY FROM THE COUNTRY
CONTROL THE JUDICIAL PROCESS
CONTROL THE CHILDREN - COMPULSORY EDUCATION
CONTROL THE COMMUNICATION PROCESS
DISPENSE WITH FREEDOM OF SPEECH
PASSPORT CONTROL
CONTROL OF MEDICAL CARE
CONTROL ACCESS TO MONEY
CONTROL THOUGHT PROCESSES
UNDERMINE MOTIVATION

The information age should have provided the world with more freedom. It is axiomatic that information can make one strive for freedom. Obviously, the suppressive governments have made successful efforts to control the information process and formulate propaganda programs.

Laws are passed that become a war on employers. Their positive elements, if any, are vastly outpaced by negative factors. Paper work requirements alone submerged many enterprises.

One of the culprits is the Sarbanes - Oxley law, which became an unnecessary challenge for U.S. businesses. In addition, other laws and regulations, many could not deal with the severity of purposeful negative actions, and had to look for a multitude of alternatives, e.g., go international for initial offerings, (like London) , or go out of business . Again we have the characteristic of overreacting to the event and not identifying the fraudulent problem as it developed. The Sarbanes-Oxley legislation was an overreacted result of the Enron crisis.

As a result of the ill contrived legislation, many hedge funds are now operating in London and not New York. Initial price offerings which are beneficial to Wall Street are now taking place in London. Changes due to government policy, which extricate businesses from the United States, are not even projected to be amended or rescinded. Are the actions intentional or do the acting powers realize the negative results of their actions?

With a multiplicity of factors being used against the Capitalistic characteristics of the country, it is not easy to search out positives.

1. Regulatory agencies taking over for courts and legislatures
2. Unmanageable deficits
3. Taxes being indiscriminately applied
4. A shrinking labor force subtraction of private sector jobs
5. Numerous Government programs which only create more government jobs
6. Stepping up of lies along with exaggerations of reality

Broken promises litter the social and economic system. Continually the number of people employed decreases. Therefore, it stands to reason that the economic policy is not working. Moreover, as the Administration continues its existence, President Obama is viewed as being more incompetent.

House minority leader, John Boehner, communicates that we will, through hard work and entrepreneurship, recover. Given the downward trend and the projected continuation of the trend, how is this possible? Of course the vast majority hope that he is right. As a result of the giant size victories at the polls for the Republicans, John Boehner will become the House majority leader, replacing Nancy Pelosi.

The projection of a plethora of taxes to take place in 2011 will have incalculable devastation effects on the economy. The redundancy or repetitiveness should not minimize the thoughts on the impact. The following data is presented by the Heritage Foundation. It is not in its entirety.

- $ 2.4 trillion as a result of the expiration of tax cuts.
- 1.5 million Jobs that won't be created as a result of the repeal of the death tax.
- Over one half a trillion dollars for a down payment on Obama care.
- The tax increases as a result of the reinstatement of the marriage penalty.
- The capitalistic system created the greatest middle class in the history of the world. It is now, with impunity, being destroyed.

It is difficult to look behind the fact that the US is being handed over, somewhat intact, by Obama, to a world banking power.

The Federal Reserve, a monstrously corrupt organization, is performing the greatest financial scam in the history of the world. The Federal Reserve is not Federal. It is a privately owned and tax exempt entity that is controlled by foreign banking interests.

Congressman Barney Frank called for the auditing of the Federal Reserve. He did this knowing that it will never happen. Of course this was a phony move on his part, maybe to make a futile attempt to separate himself from the Federal Reserve.

Jerome R. Corsi, America for Sale, outlined what needed to be accomplished in saying no to the Global New Deal:

1. Close down the Federal Reserve
2. Pull out of the trade agreements - NAFTA, CAFTA, and the WTO.
3. Close down the United Nations, the International Monetary Fund, and the World Bank
4. Cut taxes and close the IRS.
5. Create a Gold-Backed US Dollar for International Trade.

These five suggestions are well thought out. To rid the American public of these organizations would instantaneously portend improvement in both the economic and sociological outlook. However, these sinister global systems will not permit this to become a reality.

Obama is driven by accomplishing his agenda. The voters are deprived of influence. For example, he is dead set on destroying the jobs. Unemployed people are subject to government control. In his vision, United States is to exist in a world where it is subjugated to the global influence of communism and socialism. The members of Congress who were instrumental in rubber stamping his agenda, which is leading the U.S. into oblivion, are shunning him and belatedly, appear to have some understanding of the perils of his definition of change, and its corresponding effects on the voters. Many are now calling him the worst President in history. He continues undaunted, continuing to sing the praises of slow and sure improvement. Obama points to hope in the future. To communists, pointing to hope in the future is of paramount importance. After a while, the propaganda falls on deaf ears, as populace eventually loses all hope of having a decent life. The unemployed are no longer listening. His sycophants are continuing to emphasize the same failed methodologies, like continued government spending to get us out of the mess.

The victory of the Republicans at the polls translated into optimism for many Americans. One can only hope that this outlook will provide more that just hope.

Much is being made of reversing the deleterious direction by voting the culprits out of office. Not to be overlooked is that the plans and the programs of the "Agenda" have been set in motion. People to enforce the legislation are already in place as civil service employees.

The election losses brought forth a plethora of ideas as to how Obama could change course and follow a viable plan for election in 2012. One such person, David Brooks, of the New York Times, took the time and effort to write such a plan. It was editorialized in the Kansas City Star on November 3, 2010.

"The road map for Obama's recovery after Tuesdays is pretty straight-forward."

"First, the President is going to have to win back independents. Liberals are criticizing him for being too timid. But the fact is that Obama will win 99.9 percent of the liberal vote in 2012, and in a presidential year, liberal turnout will surely by high."

"Second, Obama needs to redefine his identity."

"Third, Obama will need to respond to the nation's fear of decline".

"Fourth, Obama has to build an institutional structure to support a more moderate approach".

This was laconically extracted. There is no need to elaborate. Indeed, the only purpose is to ask the question as to how these people can think that the President would even want to change course. Anything suggested along these lines would be diametrically opposed to Obama's agenda. If left to Obama, the devastation will continue. The 2010 election is over and the dilemma is continuing - unabated.

Glance at these facts:

1. There are 81 million households in the United States.
2. Over twenty million are unemployed. This is remarkably different from the daily newspaper reports.
3. Forty four million people are on food stamps.
4. The burden of providing for the excesses of government is increasingly falling on the productive citizens, and they are decreasing in number.

On the positive side, military recruitment is picking up and the tea party is increasing in its membership.

The Federal Reserve is continuing to increase the debt by creating, out of thin air, bonds and hoodwinking the citizens into believing that it is a good thing. The Fed is buying the bonds and the taxpayers will be billed for the interest. The stock market rallies on what may be perceived to be good news. This financial terrorism was tried in the past. It didn't work then, and it will not work now. In fact it will continue to feed the storm of devastation. The top risk is run away inflation. Again, it is a risk that should never be taken. It is economic idiocy. Added to all of this is $ 250. billion of unused TARP funds. Translated, it is money that will not be returned to the Treasury (taxpayer).

All of these elements have an additional sinister objective, and that is to promote negative motivation.

Now the argument or emphasis on gridlock or compromise takes on a new dimension. Obama, who avoided debate on such key issues as health care and climate change, now calls for discussions with Republicans. The last thing Socialists want is discussion or debate. Winston Churchill warned of this in 1945. Energies need to be directed toward:

1. Dismantling the health care bill
2. Revoke the recently passed consumer banking protection
3. Curtail specific operations of many of the regulatory agencies
4. Get involved in foreign policy

A) Bring some resemblances of sanity in foreign policy
B) Bring respect back to the United States
C) show leadership - allies can rely on the U.S.
D) Use the necessary force including technological resources to win the wars in Iraq and Afghanistan and curtail the bulwark actions of North Korea.

5. Work on reducing the budget expenditures - restrict or terminate some of this socialistic hand out programs.
6. Create a favorable environment for private sector jobs
7. Close the border

This is just a small portion of an endless list.

The tea party members and the majority of people like them may be the only hope for a non dictatorial future. But, unfortunately, hope within this realm appears as elusive. We need to pray for a miracle.

BIBLIOGRAPHY

AMERICA FOR SALE, Jerome R. Corsi, Simon & Schuster, Inc. New York, NY, 2009.

DOLLAR MELTDOWN, THE, Charles Goyette, Penguin Group, New York, NY, 2009.

DOW THEORY LETTERS, Richard Russell, La Jolla, Ca. June 2009, and July 2009 editions.

ENEMY WITHIN, THE, Michael Savage, WND Books, Nashville, Tn. 2003.

FAITH GIVEN ONCE, FOR ALL, THE, Charles Colson and Harold Ficket, 2008, Zordervan, Grand Rapids, Mi., 2008

JERUSALEM POST, Jerusalem, Israel, March 17, 2010. Also many other editions.

KANSAS CITY STAR. Kansas City, Missouri, November, December 2009, January, March 2010. Also many other editions.

LIMBAUGH LETTER, Radio Active Media, New York, New York, November 2009.

MAINICHI DAILY NEWS, Tokyo Japan, MARCH 2010.

MARKETING OF EVIL, THE, David Kupelian, Cumberland House Publishing, Nashville, Tn. 2005.

MIAMI HERALD, Miami, Florida, January 2010.

MONEY AND MARKETS, Dr. Martin Weiss, Internet Publication, August 2010.

NEW REPUBLIC MAGAZINE, THE, numerous articles, edition of November 4, 2009.

PAIN AND PROFIT: THE POLITICS OF MALPRACTICE, Sylvia Law and Steven Polan, Harper and Rowe, 1978.

POPE JOHN PAUL II'S Humanae Vitae, July 25, 2010 and GOOD NEWS ABOUT SEX AND MARRIAGE, by Christopher West, chapter 6, Savant Books.

PROZAC BACKLASH, Joseph Glen Mullen, M.D., Simon and Schuster, New York, 2002.

FAITH GIVEN ONCE, FOR ALL, THE, Charles Colson and Harold Ficket, 2008, Zondervan, Grand Rapids MI.2008.

S&A DIGEST: PORTER STANSBURY: October 29, 2009.

SAVAGE NATION, THE, Michael Savage, 2002, Thomas Nelson Publishers, Nashville, Tennessee.

STRAITS TIMES, Singapore, February 23, 2010.

STARS AND STRIPES, ASIAN EDITION, John R. Bolton, October 21, 2009.

WEIGHT LOSS CURE, THE, Kevin Trudeau, Alliance Publishing Group, Elk Grove Village, IL. 2009.

www.ingramcontent.com/pod-product-compliance
Lightning Source LLC
Chambersburg PA
CBHW050118280326
41933CB00010B/1153